THINKING THROUGH THE PRINCIPALSHIP

Dianne E. Ashby

Samuel E. Krug

EYE ON EDUCATION
6 DEPOT WAY WEST, SUITE 106
LARCHMONT, NY 10538
(914) 833–0551
(914) 833–0761 fax

For information about permission to reproduce selections from this book, write: Eye On Education, Permissions Dept., Suite 106, 6 Depot Way West, Larchmont, NY 10538.

ISBN 1-883001-50-1

Library of Congress Cataloging-in-Publication Data

Ashby, Dianne E., 1953–

Thinking through the principalship / Dianne E. Ashby, Samuel E. Krug

p.   cm.

Includes bibliographical references (p.).

ISBN 1-883001-50-1

1. School principals—United States. 2. School management and organization—United States. 3. Educational leadership—United States. I. Krug, Samuel E. II. Title

LB2831.92.A4   1998

371.2'012—dc21   97-42924

                                                        CIP

10 9 8 7 6 5 4 3 2 1

Editorial and production services provided by Richard H. Adin Freelance Editorial Services, 9 Orchard Drive, Gardiner, NY 12525 (914-883-5884)

What should an effective principal know and be able to do?

The answers, of course, are within the pages of this book. You can assess the extent to which you have already acquired the skills and knowledge of an effective principal by using the self-analysis worksheet beginning on page 14 of the text.

THE SCHOOL LEADERSHIP LIBRARY

A set of 21 "domains," or building blocks, representing the essential knowledge and skills of successful principals were developed by members of the National Policy Board for Educational Administration (sponsored by NCPEA, UCEA, NAESP, NASSP, ASCD, AASA and other professional organizations). David A. Erlandson and Alfred P. Wilson, General Editors, worked with a prestigious, experienced team of authors to explain and apply each building block, creating the SCHOOL LEADERSHIP LIBRARY.

Each volume in the SCHOOL LEADERSHIP LIBRARY (the list of volumes begins on page iv) includes practical materials such as:

- ◆ checklists
- ◆ sample letters and memos
- ◆ model forms
- ◆ action plans

If you are interested in ordering the SCHOOL LEADERSHIP LIBRARY, contact Eye On Education.

ABOUT THE AUTHORS

Dr. Dianne Ashby has been a teacher or administrator in middle schools, high schools, for the correctional system, and in higher education. She has written articles for the *Journal of Staff Development*, *The High School Journal*, and other publications. Dr. Ashby currently serves as Chair of the Department of Educational Administration and Foundations at Illinois State University and as Executive Director of Illinois Women Administrators.

Dr. Samuel E. Krug, the author of approximately 100 articles, books, chapters, and tests, is an adjunct professor at the University of Illinois at Urbana-Champaign where he was affiliated for many years with the National Center for School Leadership. A specialist in assessment and measurement, he is currently the president of MetriTech, Inc., a leader in educational and psychological testing, and Industrial Psychology International, Ltd., the publisher of employee selection and evaluation tests.

TABLE OF CONTENTS

INTRODUCTION

Very few people are born experts. During his school years, Einstein's teachers had significant doubts about his ability to make it in the world. Even in Mozart's case, you wonder if he would indeed have written his first composition at age five if he had not had the luxury of a composer-teacher for a father and ever-present role model. Instead of being born, experts evolve. A process by which people evolve into expert principals is the focus of this book.

After advising of the word's origins in the Latin verb *experior*, the dictionary defines the adjectival form of expert as "practiced" or "skillful." Then, in true dictionary, tautological fashion, it goes on to define the noun form as "one expert in something" or "an authority." What does it mean to be practiced or skillful at the principalship? What is there to practice? What are the skills? The problem is particularly acute because the current state of education in America does not leave much time for on-the-job training.

The dictionary is singularly unhelpful about how people become expert. Practice doesn't seem to be enough. Just ask any parent of a child who has endured daily sessions on the piano or, worse yet, the violin. After several years of lessons and regular practice, most young students still seem several lifetimes away from the *Emperor Concerto*, no matter how well they may have mastered *Für Elise*. Just increasing the practice time from one hour a day at the keyboard to six hours isn't enough to create a Horowitz. So, practice isn't sufficient. There must be another path toward "skillful."

The "authority" definition has its own problems. The biggest is probably that we tend to confuse "authority" with knowledge. Authorities on various topics are presumed to know a great deal about their topic. Economic authorities like John Maynard Keynes were able to understand and explain the causes of the Great Depression of the 1930s. Interestingly, however, it took an economic nonauthority like Franklin Roosevelt to do much about turning the Depression around. So, just knowing the answer may not be enough, either.

If we step outside the principalship for a moment, we can see this distinction between knowledge and expertise clearly at work when comparing new drivers with experienced drivers. New drivers tend to know many, often arcane and unusual, facts about driving, information that is presumably required to obtain a license. They *know* the proper distance to maintain between one vehicle and the vehicle in front. They *know* the speed limits under different kinds of conditions. They *recognize* different kinds of signs, at least on the test. They are *able to distinguish* the accelerator from the brake. However, even with all this knowledge, their on-the-road experience is usually painful at first. On the other hand, few of us who have driven an automobile very long can quickly recite the proper formula for intervehicular distance, but we usually maintain it. We may not know exactly at what point in an intersection to begin a turn, but we usually don't scrape the rear wheels on the curb while doing so.

This is one of those rare times the Latin dictionary may be of more help than the English dictionary. There, we find that one of *experior*'s meanings is "to know by experience." This suggests being expert requires an interaction between knowledge and practice, neither being sufficient alone. That important combination—knowledge earned by experience and experience shaped by knowledge—we believe is the key to what makes some principals provide extraordinary leadership to their schools. It is leadership that clearly exceeds what practice, superior management skills, the best intentions, or even being a very good person who cares about kids could solely explain.

Intelligence, skills, good intentions, and caring attitudes are desirable, but each alone, or even in combination, is not enough. Our rapidly changing world makes rigorous and high stakes demands on schools and their leaders. Expert principals must be able to try new solutions and reflect on their experiences. They must think reflectively, collaboratively, strategically, and critically. They must be able to combine their thinking abilities with excellent skills, ethical intentions, and understanding of schools as organizations. Expert principals are uniquely able to manage the ambiguity of a job that requires them to lead their schools as complex interrelated systems of people, structures, purposes, and motives at the same time that they must be prepared to deal with each individual or group's short- and long-term agendas.

The purpose of this book is to provide new and aspiring principals with insights into how principals who have become experts at school leadership think about their schools and the ways in which what they do impacts their schools. It is about basics, but not those basics you should know from introductory graduate coursework, internships, and rudimentary in-service programs (for example, school law, budget, scheduling, meetings). Instead, this book is about the basics of thinking about what you do, how you do it, and perhaps most important, why you do it. It is about thinking of your school as a unified whole that cannot be defined by listing its parts and using that perspective to forge the best possible education for your ultimate responsibility, our children.

This book is organized so that you can compare your development with a framework of important ways of thinking and behaving with the intention of helping you develop your style in the principalship. This is one area in which we disagree with those who would appear to suggest that there are "ten easy steps" or "five fundamental skills" or "seven essential habits" of successful leaders.

There may be some skills that are fundamental to school leadership, but we're not sure how many there are or exactly what they might be. There may be certain essential habits, but we can't for the life of us think of what they might be, let alone count them. Our reflections on highly effective principals suggest instead that there is no skill pattern that clearly differentiates expert from inexpert leadership of schools. Of course, leaders must be able to communicate. But our observation is that they do so in many different ways. For example, some communicate their excitement about reading to younger students by holding reading contests; others communicate their sense of reading's importance by ensuring that the library is well stocked and easily accessible to students. Some regularly communicate the school's educational mission through newsletters, assemblies, and other formal channels. Others do so by meeting the school bus in the morning and inviting students into the school. Some of the expert principals we have seen are flamboyant and dynamic; others are quiet and purposeful. In short, we have often noted the diverse ways that individuals provide expert leadership in school buildings. After reflection, we have come to the conclusion that it's not so much what some principals do that causes them to be regarded as experts in the role. Rather, it is in the reasoning behind what they do and the purposes underlying their varied activities that we have come to discover greater communality about what makes an expert principal.

This book provides a framework for thinking about the role of leadership in the school. Consequently, it is about the role of the principal within the school. Part I examines social, political, and professional pressures on the principal. It describes the role of modern principals and explores reasons highly intelligent and giving people continue to be attracted to what is often, at best, a terribly ambiguous role, filled with increasingly uncertain demands.

Part I also introduces two principals whose struggles with how to best lead their schools are integrated throughout the book. Nick Freeman is the new principal of Whitney Elementary School. Whitney is part of a large city system. Nick began his teaching career at Whitney and is dedicated to the students and the community. Nick finds himself somewhat frustrated with the ways in which relationships are unfolding now that he is a principal rather than a teacher. Past administrators and long-time teachers have left undone the important work of minimizing conflict and maximizing learning opportunities in the face of a rapidly changing student population. The story of Central High School and its principal Elizabeth Harris also unfolds as the book progresses. Elizabeth is a caring, competent administrator. Yet her first year at Central left her dissatisfied. Too often she felt reactive rather than proactive. Too many unplanned and unforeseen circumstances, most of them preventable, demanded precious time. Elizabeth determined that she should not spend her second year as a reactor. She would become more strategic. Both Nick and Elizabeth appear throughout the book as they wrestle with issues of educational mission, school climate, curriculum management, staff supervision, and student learning.

This book is about becoming expert in your own principalship. It is about thinking through what you believe and how you behave so that you and your school may achieve the congruence necessary for systemic school improvement. This book is not about organization or political theory. Even so, growth in leadership expertise requires awareness of the forces, past, present, and future, that make the job simultaneously exciting and exasperating. Ever since Americans abandoned the one-room schoolhouse for schools with separated grade levels, a configuration often described as isolated classrooms joined by a common parking lot, the principal has served as the human connection among classrooms and between the classrooms and other agencies. This role is assumed to be a vital one, if for no other reason than that internal and external constituencies have a readily identifiable complaint department. Beyond that, just what vital function the principal performs has been the subject of vigorous debate. Disciplinarian, activity scheduler, central office liaison, records manager, budget analyst, facilitator, public relations expert, head learner. The roles are as varied as the people who have attempted to analyze and describe them.

Part I also introduces a framework of behaviors and practices identified by research as characteristic of effective principals. This part of the book includes self-assessment tools designed to help you think reflectively about your school and your leadership.

Part II describes a framework of research-based perspectives, skills, and behaviors practiced by highly effective principals and provides guides to enriching your own viewpoint, skills, and behaviors. It describes each of five dimensions that provide a structure for thinking about the role of leadership in schools. Each dimension represents measurable and observable characteristics of schools led by effective and expert principals.

However, as we said earlier, we don't want to confuse the structure of this framework with a simple "five-step plan" to building wellness. The framework provides language for our discussion of ideas, thoughts, and behaviors that should not be sorted and separated as neatly as the words imply. The dimensions transcend school contexts, and school contexts differ significantly. This requires principals to adapt the framework to fit them and their schools. Also, it is important to realize that although the framework has been divided into five dimensions for purposes of discussion, none is mutually exclusive. They messily overlap, affect each other, and blend. In the same way, expert principals don't easily compartmentalize the ways they think about schools. Each plan, relationship, or critical decision blends imperceptibly into others. Nothing occurs in isolation in schools. Everything affects something else.

Schools have always needed strategic, artful, expert principals. Principals' concerns, however, have changed over the years. Part III challenges you to expand the ways you think about the impact of school leadership, particularly ways that involve reflection, collaboration, and strategy.

Increasing emphasis in the past quarter century on the school as the unit of change has shifted the roles of both superintendents and principals. Site-based management as an approach to running school districts has changed the relationships between principals and central offices, between principals and teachers, and between principals and the families they serve. Relying on traditional ways of thinking and working a task at a time won't enable principals to envision the future, entice others to participate in making that vision reality, create a climate for learning, guide curriculum, monitor student progress, supervise staff, and organize the details of the daily work of schools. Principals have to become mental jugglers.

Few principals can put in more time. Instead they must plan, build relationships, and problem solve so that they leverage the energy of the school to make things happen. Expert principals understand that theory and practice are not mutually exclusive. Rather, expert principals use theory and practice to inform each other and to move their schools. Part III challenges principals to stretch their abilities to think, plan, build relationships, and problem solve. The final chapter emphasizes the importance of integrating your ways of thinking with each other and with your own moral code.

Consider reading this book as a joint exercise with a trusted colleague whom you know is just as interested in becoming an expert as you are. Use the self-assessments and experiences of the principals profiled throughout the book as starting points for your conversations about the process. You might consider beginning an informal journal. It can be something as simple as a ring binder in which you write answers to the self assessments and record thoughts about why you selected the answers you did. The journal can also serve as a means of comparing and contrasting your approach to events of each school day with practices you would like to adopt.

PART I

THE PRINCIPAL AS SCHOOL LEADERSHIP EXPERT

1

New Expectations for the Principalship?

It used to be that we thought the principal's office was a place where you went only if you were sent. If you were sent, good luck! Your parents might still love you, although it would take time to heal the shame. Your teacher would take you back, although that relationship would never be quite the same again. Students would look at you differently, a mixture of awe and pity in their faces. After all, you were someone who returned from where few had gone.

Like Randall Flagg in Steven King's novel *The Stand*, the principal was the "dark man" of the school. We assumed that the principal's job was essentially the same as Torquemada's, Spain's 15th century inquisitor-general—the destruction of heretics. Not one of us believed for a moment the old mnemonic for keeping the two homonyms straight: there was no way the principal was our "pal."

The announcement in 1983 that we were a "nation at risk" and that our system of public education rested on the edge of destruction startled many Americans. However, the real shocker came later when researchers began to examine schools that appeared to be especially effective at educating students. These schools were distinguished by a large number of characteristics. Among the most important was the pivotal role played by their principals.

The diehards among us at first assumed that these schools had finally consolidated the principal's office and furnace room, thus freeing space for libraries and laboratories where real learning could occur. This seemed a reasonable assumption considering that these were the two scariest places in the building. In addition, we assumed that the two positions, principal and custodian, had at last been economically merged into a single position, the "princodian" or "custipal," thus freeing funds for additional instructional staff. After all, the two jobs appeared to overlap substantially. Both seemed somehow to involve maintenance.

We were wrong. It wasn't the elimination of the principals from these schools but rather their reemergence that distinguished these schools. These principals were alive and well and they were doing something more than suppressing heretics. They were actually playing a proactive role in the instructional process. They were, in fact, leaders of instruction.

TODAY'S PRINCIPAL

As a principal, you are continually under a microscope. Even people who applaud your long work hours will criticize you for not working hard enough when you don't return their phone calls within the hour or when your answering machine picks up at home (regardless of the hour). Every aspect of your school, from the clutter left behind stage by the orchestra to the performance of athletic teams (including who makes the team, who plays, and who sits on the bench) to student achievement (including college entrance test scores and disputes over whether a student earned an A- or a B+), are considered your responsibility because they happen on your watch.

Until the mid-1970s, the principal's job was clearly, although somewhat more narrowly, defined. Principals performed three key roles: building manager, student disciplinarian, and line officer for the superintendent's office. Efficient building management meant managing custodians, directing office staff to order books and supplies, developing a class schedule, keeping the books balanced, overseeing the Fall opening of the building, as well as special events, athletic contests, and the end of school. Disciplining students required annual meetings with staff to revise school rules and sanctions for violations. Throughout the year the principal and assistant principal would see students about behaviors ranging from chewing gum and being tardy to fighting and skipping school. Patrolling parking lots and bathrooms for smokers took as much of the high school principal's time as did calling parents to report misbehavior. Carrying out orders from the superintendent's office was sometimes unpleasant, but seldom difficult. After all, the principal was only doing what he (usually "he") was told, which was the only choice most school employees thought they had (and the only choice the superintendent *knew* they had). More technical issues like hiring, budgeting, staff development, and curriculum were, for the most part, a central office function and of little or no direct concern to the principal.

In these good old days, teachers taught, principals managed the buildings, and students were assumed commodities. Principals knew who the good teachers were, and systematically visited (or ignored if that was more politically expedient) the classrooms of teachers they knew were bad. Principals kept buildings open so that educational opportunities could be broadly provided. If, like the proverbial horse led to water who would not drink, some students chose not to learn, they were often ignored. In time they just faded away.

This isn't to say that principals of past decades didn't do a good job. They did the job that was expected, and they did it well. Today's principals face more complex expectations forged by a very different student population and a new generation dissatisfied with the educational status quo. At a time when many view the schools as one of the few intact social organizations, students come with very different attitudes, motivations, and needs than students of generations past. Past generations of principals needed largely to serve as administrators of a commodity—learning—perceived as valuable and desirable by most students. Today's principals often need to find ways of inducing students to learn despite their most ardent attempts to escape.

GLOBAL INFLUENCES ON A LOCAL ROLE

The principalship is a locally controlled position. School governance rests primarily in the hands of locally elected or appointed school boards. School personnel are approved for hiring, firing, reappointment, and tenure by those school boards. Administrators of appropriate rank may handle personnel evaluations, but they are subject to board scrutiny.

Principals, whose actions are always subject to school board review, are hired to lead schools established by boards to serve defined populations of children. These may be neighborhood schools, schools integrated by busing, magnet schools, alternative schools, or schools defined by grade clusters. Most of the concerns of principals as they perform their daily duties are local in nature, such as student attendance, student discipline, teacher performance, student and teacher safety, school–home communications, and community relations. In some cases, local concerns place enormous burdens on schools when they serve children living within communities where crime, violence, addiction, poverty, and disease are the rule rather than the exception. Local politics can make the principalship uncomfortable as fiscal, social, political, and religious groups seek to influence the budget, curriculum, governance, and purpose of schools.

Although principals clearly affect and are affected by local concerns of varying consequences, today's principals must realize also that their influence and the factors influencing them go far beyond local boundaries. We are living at a time when the world figuratively shrinks and knowledge expands with each technological advancement. Satellites that first made global telecommunication reliable and economical also provided an infrastructure for the information superhighway. The fax explosion of the 1980s and related communication services like e-mail removed communication barriers created by differences in clocks around the world. As a practical matter, these rapid changes in our science and technology mean there are new things to learn each day. Literacy means something very different today than it did at the turn of the last century. Schools, and the principals who lead them into the next century, must adapt to different roles, different needs, and different strategies. The local role requires global understanding.

We have clearly moved from the agrarian and industrial models familiar to most of us to an undefined age filled with new demands for information. Tom Peters is an organizational guru whose books have been read almost as avidly by educators as by business people. Peters suggests that in a knowledge-driven economy, workers must behave very differently than they did when the assembly line was king. Conversation will not be seen as a distraction but as a work tool, and will take many forms, many of those forms shaped by new communication technologies. Even the idea of "going to work" is changing as more and more people work out of homes and hotels rather than from centralized headquarters (Peters, 1994).

As information becomes the coin of new world markets, technologies for creating and accessing information require new structures for living and learning. In the same way that these technologies have redefined our notion of work, they may equally well redefine our notion of communities and of schools. Schools must prepare students for a new world of work that requires skill in new forms of conversation. Schools must also plan for continuous changes in the nature of schooling that are a natural concomitant of continuous changes in the nature of living. Schools will always be in the business of culturally and intellectually educating new generations, but the means of doing that business will constantly change.

At the same time that technological innovations shrink our world, rapidly deteriorating economic and social conditions in many areas bring us closer together in the fight for human dignity and life. Students don't look or act as they did just a few short years ago. This is perhaps most noticeable in big city schools that now serve diverse populations very different from those a generation past. However, cultural diversity has come to suburban and rural districts as well. Schools used to serving homogeneous populations with common backgrounds strive to serve heterogeneous populations from diverse backgrounds and with complicated and disparate needs. City schools most particularly, but even schools in areas insulated before the communication revolution, wrestle with the deadly impact of alcohol, drugs, and violence.

Education critics emphasize that the economic and social well-being of future generations requires that schools successfully educate increasingly demanding populations. The cost of failures is so high that society simply cannot afford to discard some students. In tune with these critiques and motivated by concern for their children, parents demand new relationships with schools.

Not all these messages are clear. On the one hand, business supports schools with partnerships, internships, and intergenerational education. On the other hand, business often opposes the flow of resources to school systems by demanding tax incentives and opposing increased taxes targeted toward school improvement. Parents also seem to send simultaneous contradictory messages to schools. On the one hand, they want individualized services and considerations for their children, yet they push for control over the curriculum and limitation of administrator and teacher efforts to shape student behavior. Principals face these paradoxes daily as the front line leaders of local schools.

CHANGING AMERICAN EDUCATION

Change in schools is nothing new. American schools have historically responded to the needs of communities they serve. Nevertheless, and despite a tradition of local control, national issues have increasingly influenced schools during the current century. During its opening decades, schools responded to the influx of immigrants, predominantly European, by teaching their children to assimilate, to become "American." When electronics later redefined the American way of life and Russia's 1957 launch of Sputnik caused Americans to see scientific and technical education as essential for national survival, schools quickly adapted. "New math" emerged alongside science education in elementary schools and advanced science courses in high schools. Small districts consolidated to use limited resources more effectively. Federal funding led to the design and dissemination of innovative programs that emphasized teacher preparation and staff development.

At one time, the primary purpose of schooling was assumed to be to prepare a citizenry for the responsibilities of democracy. Although many hope this remains a priority for schools, it seems that schools have changed throughout U.S. history, not in response to increased demands for literate citizens but in response to changing demands related to economic survival and competitiveness. As the twentieth century evolved, work shifted from entrepreneurial agrarians to factory work, shifted again to service providers, and now appears to be shifting to communications specializations. The education of a high-potential workforce has become more clearly articulated as a primary purpose of schooling. Although schools have long prepared people for work, the cost of failures increases in proportion to the technical requirements of jobs. There were many more opportunities available to men and women with limited reading skills, for example, at the turn of the century than there are now. The probability that they could survive independently was much higher then than now.

Energized by *A Nation at Risk*, which the Commission on Excellence in Education published in 1983, federal and state governments attempted to raise the academic bar and hold schools increasingly accountable for the quality of the education they provided. In response, many schools developed new standards and expectations for students. Simultaneously, they began to consider new ways of defining and organizing the work of administrators, teachers, and students.

Not everyone joined the bandwagon immediately. Some school administrators took the position that "this, too, shall pass," which it does with astonishing regularity in a field where "significant" reforms occur about as often as holidays. Others took the position that, as professionals, they didn't need to respond to lay concerns. Unfortunately for them, education is the one field in which nearly everyone has experience. Educators who ignored public opinion, business pressure, and political leverage found that circling the wagons was ineffective against sophisticated and high tech assaults. Some members of the community, impatient with the pace of reform, took matters into their own hands, creating home schooling networks, charter schools, voucher plans, and other alternatives to traditional schooling. However, many public school administrators embraced the challenge and took calls for creating effective schools seriously. They became the center of school reform.

NEW EXPECTATIONS OF PRINCIPALS

Much has been written about what principals in schools that are effective by contemporary standards do. The Ohio State Leadership Studies of the 1940s represented one of the first attempts to examine the effectiveness of school administrators. They defined effectiveness in terms of providing teachers with a structured and considerate work setting (Hoy & Miskel, 1987). Over time, administrator effectiveness became a more central topic of debate. In the early 1970s, the term "instructional leadership" emerged to describe administrative, supportive, coordinating, and initiating roles (Brieve, 1972), all revolving around the principal addressing the workplace needs of teachers. Research in schools that managed to succeed despite overwhelming societal challenges tied principal functions directly to student achievement. Teachers in 22 Emergency School Aid Act (ESAA) schools said their principals provided administrative leadership in instruction, coordinated instructional programs, and emphasized high academic standards (Marcus, 1976; Wellisch, MacQueen, Carriere, & Duck,

1978). Other studies by Weber (1971), Edmonds (1979), and Brookover et al. (1982) found that principals of effective schools set the tone for the schools, assumed responsibility for instruction, and made themselves available to teachers and students.

Effective schools research of the 1970s unintentionally signaled the reemergence of principals as essential to schools at the same time that the Carnegie Report and some teacher groups sought to minimize the position. But the principals featured in effective schools research were different from their colleagues who managed less effective schools. Principals of effective schools played a proactive role in the instructional process. At the top of his list of characteristics that distinguished effective schools, Austin (1979) noted that the schools had a stated purpose or mission. Principals of effective schools clearly communicated that purpose to teachers, students, and parents. In these schools, leaders had forged a clear educational mission from loose confederations of classrooms and corridors. This was particularly important for student populations that were increasingly diverse both in their cultures and their needs.

The National Policy Board for Educational Administration worked with ten national organizations to identify a knowledge and skill base for the principalship. The organizations represented school administrators at all levels and university professors working with preparation programs. The Board intended for this work to "provide a platform for practice" and to address core professional responsibilities so that persons qualifying for practice could fulfill essential tasks in various contexts (National Policy Board, 1993). The intent was also to create a genuine link between the knowledge base of university professors who study schools and the knowledge base of practicing school administrators.

The knowledge and skills identified by the Board are the result of two processes: an inductive task analysis and a deductive theoretical analysis. The 21 domains the Board defined are not presumed to be of equal importance nor distinct. The overlap is intentional. It stems from a realization that the principalship consists of overlapping skills and knowledge. Descriptions of each are accompanied in the Board's latest publication by a literature review, performance standards, recommendations for education and training development, and recommendations for evaluation of skills. The National Council for Teacher Education and the National Policy Board have collaborated with many state education agencies to develop guidelines universities may use when integrating these domains into their principal preparation programs. The domains are listed here with brief explanations.

NATIONAL POLICY BOARD FOR EDUCATIONAL ADMINISTRATION STANDARDS FOR THE PRINCIPALSHIP

I. FUNCTIONAL DOMAINS

1. Leadership (vision, culture, improvement)

2. Information Collection (problem solving through identifying, collecting, analyzing, and presenting data)

3. Problem Analysis (recognizing problems, systematic analysis of problems, barriers to problem solution, information collection and analysis, solution finding)

4. Judgment (thinking skills, organizing information, integrating information, reaching logical conclusions, controlling emotions and bias, using reflection)

5. Organizational Oversight (translating vision to planning, working with groups, defining roles and relationships, using decision-making tools, patterns of decision making, evaluation)

6. Implementation (scheduling events, anticipating problems, monitoring progress, evaluation, single-loop and double-loop learning)

7. Delegation (strategies, problems, communication, organization, monitoring, risk taking)

II. PROGRAMMATIC DOMAINS

8. Instruction and the Learning Environment (effective practices, research on instruction, assisting teachers, learning styles, classroom strategies, scheduling, school organization, measurement and evaluation, analysis of test data, supervisory techniques)

9. Curriculum Design (role of principals, evaluation, written vs. taught vs. tested curriculum, organizational models, mapping, alignment, evaluation, needs assessment)

10. Student Guidance and Development (student growth and development, counseling, and student activities)

11. Staff Development (program development, mentoring, coaching, conferencing, needs assessment, evaluation)

12. Measurement and Evaluation (evaluating student outcomes, linking assessment and curriculum, designing accountability mechanisms, policy implications)

13. Resource Allocation (resource allocation systems, linking resources and goals, district and nondistrict sources, procurement, monitoring, building budget, technical procedures, inventory, purchasing)

III. INTERPERSONAL DOMAINS

14. Motivating Others (teamwork, collegiality, participative decision making, staff autonomy, parents, feedback, productivity, rewards)

15. Interpersonal Sensitivity (interpersonal relations, observation skills, managing conflict, seeking information, recognition)

16. Oral and Nonverbal Expression (effective behaviors, articulation and work choice, listening, feedback, various audiences, cultural and gender factors, small and large group presentations, media technology)

17. Written Expression (four-stage writing process, job specific documents, feedback, computer technology)

IV. CONTEXTUAL DOMAINS

18. Philosophical and Cultural Values (self-awareness, judgment, values and conflicts in American education, diversity of values, various philosophical perspectives, socially constructed reality)

19. Legal and Regulatory Applications (constitutional rights, federal statutory and regulatory provisions, state constitutional, statutory, and regulatory provisions, civil and criminal liability, contracts, grants, and financial accounts)

20. Policy and Political influences (political systems and schools, formal and informal political relationships, policy theory, political strategies, power relationships, political interests, ethical principles)

21. Public Relations (public relations plans, internal and external audiences, mass and interpersonal communications, target groups, message strategies, opinion leaders, news coverage, crisis, communications technologies)

We join Roland Barth (1990) in his disdain of list logic. Listing what makes a good principal provides important information. However, lists poorly capture the essence of what makes a principal great (Barth, 1990).

Nevertheless, the NPBEA list provides a useful perspective on important aspects of the principalship, and we will use it as a first stimulus for self-assessment. Begin reflecting on your work as a principal now by assessing the extent to which you have acquired these skills and knowledge. Use the worksheet we have prepared to do that. This isn't a sophisticated instrument but a stimulus for self-reflection. Its value to you lies in your frankness and honesty. Evaluate yourself in each domain by selecting a value between "1" and "5." A "1" means that your knowledge of the area and your skills have considerable room for development. By contrast, a rating of "5" means that you believe your knowledge is fairly extensive and your skills are well developed.

To assist you in making your ratings, we have included a set of "issues to consider" as you evaluate yourself. These are questions you might ask yourself to help you position yourself on each scale. The more often you find yourself giving positive answers to the questions, the more likely a higher numeric rating is appropriate. The more frequently you find yourself confused by the question or answering negatively, the more likely a lower rating is appropriate. Again, this is not a sophisticated instrument but a stimulus for reflection. Give yourself a reasonable amount of time to consider each area, but don't worry yourself to death. Your first impression is likely to be your best assessment.

WORKSHEET FOR SELF-ANALYSIS ON PRINCIPALSHIP KNOWLEDGE AND SKILLS

Leadership

1- - - - - 2- - - - - 3- - - - - 4- - - - - 5
Undeveloped   Refined

Issues to Consider: I have a well-developed educational philosophy I share with others. I can get groups of people to agree and to accomplish important tasks. I am a good role model; my actions are those of a good educator and others try to be like me. I visualize the future and strategize ways to move my school toward that future.

Information Collection

1- - - - - 2- - - - - 3- - - - - 4- - - - - 5
Undeveloped   Refined

Issues to Consider: I seek tangible and relevant data before making important decisions. I investigate a variety of sources before making important decisions. I use technology to collect and process information.

Problem Analysis

1- - - - - 2- - - - - 3- - - - - 4- - - - - 5
Undeveloped   Refined

Issues to Consider: I avoid implementing a solution until I thoroughly understand the problem. I generate more than one hypothesis for the cause of a problem. I generate more than one possible and workable solution.

Judgment

1- - - - - 2- - - - - 3- - - - - 4- - - - - 5
Undeveloped   Refined

Issues to Consider: I effectively forecast whether something will be a real problem. I discriminate between information that is reliable, of high quality, and of importance from that which is misleading, false, or inconsequential. I reach conclusions based on logic. I store and recall information at a level sufficient to make effective decisions.

Organizational Oversight

1- - - - - 2- - - - - 3- - - - - 4- - - - - 5

Undeveloped   Refined

Issues to Consider: I work with others to develop and implement short- and long-range plans. I abandon work that distracts from the goals of the organization. I understand and use several strategies for managing and monitoring multiple long-range projects.

Implementation

1- - - - - 2- - - - - 3- - - - - 4- - - - - 5

Undeveloped   Refined

Issues to Consider: I make things happen and others want to participate. I understand and use various approaches to organizational change. I believe that midcourse corrections are sometimes necessary and desirable.

Delegation

1- - - - - 2- - - - - 3- - - - - 4- - - - - 5

Undeveloped   Refined

Issues to Consider: I allow and expect others to be part of the decision-making and action-taking team. I am clear about my expectations regarding the authority and responsibility others in the organization have for acceptably completing tasks.

Instructional Program

1- - - - - 2- - - - - 3- - - - - 4- - - - - 5

Undeveloped   Refined

Issues to Consider: I recognize that children's learning needs differ. I make decisions based on how their consequences will affect student learning. I involve professionals, support staff, and parents in creating a positive learning environment for students.

Curriculum Design

1- - - - - 2- - - - - 3- - - - - 4- - - - - 5

Undeveloped   Refined

Issues to Consider: I work with others to align curriculum and assessment across grade levels. I work with others to constantly monitor social and technological developments for ways they might affect the curriculum.

Student Guidance and Development

1- - - - - 2- - - - - 3- - - - - 4- - - - - 5

Undeveloped   Refined

Issues to Consider: I believe the school should find ways to provide guidance, counseling, and auxiliary services to students. I work with others to find ways to connect schooling with plans for adult life. I work with others to link school-sponsored activities with learning.

Staff Development

1- - - - - 2- - - - - 3- - - - - 4- - - - - 5

Undeveloped   Refined

Issues to Consider: I have experience assessing development needs of teachers and other staff. I have experience designing and implementing learning experiences for adults. I know how to align individual development needs and organizational needs to create effective and efficient staff development programs.

Measurement and Evaluation

1- - - - - 2- - - - - 3- - - - - 4- - - - - 5

Undeveloped   Refined

Issues to Consider: I gather and use appropriate data to determine needs of students, staff, and the school. I work with others to establish standards, to measure progress toward meeting standards, and to revise instructional programs appropriately.

Resource Allocation

1- - - - - 2- - - - - 3- - - - - 4- - - - - 5

Undeveloped   Refined

Issues to Consider: I work with others to develop realistic budgets. I find ways to balance the budget despite changing conditions throughout the year. I work with others to find ways to share resources.

Motivating Others

1- - - - - 2- - - - - 3- - - - - 4- - - - - 5
Undeveloped   Refined

Issues to Consider: I can get others to build a commitment to a course of action. I recognize and reward the performance of others. I support and reinforce appropriate innovations.

Sensitivity

1- - - - - 2- - - - - 3- - - - - 4- - - - - 5
Undeveloped   Refined

Issues to Consider: I perceive the needs and concerns of others quickly. I am tactful. I work with others in emotionally stressful situations to reduce conflicts. I adapt my approach to my audiences.

Oral Expression

1- - - - - 2- - - - - 3- - - - - 4- - - - - 5
Undeveloped   Refined

Issues to Consider: I make clear and easy-to-understand presentations. I ask clarifying questions. I summarize on behalf of the group. I listen as well as I talk.

Written Expression

1- - - - - 2- - - - - 3- - - - - 4- - - - - 5
Undeveloped   Refined

Issues to Consider: I express ideas clearly in writing. I write appropriately for different audiences. I can prepare concise but considerate memoranda.

Philosophical and Cultural Values

1- - - - - 2- - - - - 3- - - - - 4- - - - - 5
Undeveloped   Refined

Issues to Consider: I recognize philosophical and historical influences on education. I understand the reciprocal influences of education and culture. I have a well-defined personal philosophy of the role of education in society. I operate within a well-defined ethical system.

Legal and Regulatory Applications

1 - - - - - 2 - - - - - 3 - - - - - 4 - - - - - 5

Undeveloped   **Refined**

Issues to Consider: I act according to laws, rules, and policies relevant to schools. I recognize governmental influences on education. I understand how to administer contracts. I use a reliable resource to remain current regarding important court decisions that affect building-level decisions.

Policy and Political Influences

1 - - - - - 2 - - - - - 3 - - - - - 4 - - - - - 5

Undeveloped   **Refined**

Issues to Consider: I identify public policy issues that affect education. I work through professional and public groups to promote policies related to student welfare.

Public and Media Relationships

1 - - - - - 2 - - - - - 3 - - - - - 4 - - - - - 5

Undeveloped   **Refined**

Issues to Consider: I work with media to develop informed perceptions about school issues. I interact effectively with parental and community opinion leaders. I respond skillfully to electronic and printed news media. I initiate news reports about my school.

SELF-REFLECTION ON THE PRINCIPALSHIP: INTRODUCING NICK FREEMAN

From the time he was a high school junior, Nick Freeman knew that he wanted to be an elementary school teacher. He enjoyed the sophomore English project that required advanced English students to "adopt" a third grader with whom they read and later wrote an original book. During his junior and senior years, Nick convinced the other students on the high school newspaper staff to work with fifth graders and their teachers to publish a newspaper. Although it was probably apparent to others, Nick didn't actually voice his desire to be an elementary teacher. The rest of the basketball team might not understand, and he didn't want to be kidded.

Nick's sense of isolation regarding his career choice decreased only slightly when he attended university. Hundreds of elementary education majors filled foundation-level lecture halls. Small pockets of two or three males sitting together dotted the assemblies. Looking on the bright side, Nick figured he was not only getting to study for the career of his choice, but his major provided great opportunities to meet women. He also hoped that his mother's belief that being a male elementary education major would not stigmatize him as weird but would, instead, be an advantage when he began looking for a job.

It was no surprise that Nick had little trouble finding an elementary position upon graduation. His minor in science education was a real bonus to city schools eager to hire male role models to lead their elementary classrooms. Several schools in the large city wanted Nick. Nick picked Whitney, a small school with a good reputation for working with children and their families. Despite desegregation-inspired busing, more than half the students attending Whitney walked to school, continuing a tradition of community-school cooperation. Most of the teachers had spent their entire careers at Whitney. They knew and had the respect of multiple generations of the same families. A teacher showing up on the home doorstep to report on a child's school performance was not unusual in the least. At Whitney, Nick learned about meeting children's needs and communicating with parents about school. He learned to adjust lessons and address emotional and physical needs before expecting young children to stretch intellectually. In his first six years at Whitney, Nick taught fourth grade, third grade, and second grade. He loved his work.

Even as Nick was learning about the importance of community to Whitney's success with students, the school was changing to reflect changes in both the neighborhoods surrounding Whitney and the city as a whole. Whitney's minority student population gradually changed from primarily black faces to increasingly tan and brown faces. The first new faces were Asian, primarily Vietnamese and then Korean. They were followed closely by Spanish-speaking students and their families. Mini cultural wars began springing up on sidewalks in front of homes. The oldest students, sixth graders, carried the antagonisms of adolescents and adults from the streets to Whitney's playgrounds and hallways.

Nick began working on a master's degree during his second year at Whitney. His motivation stemmed initially from a desire to progress on the salary schedule, and a local university conveniently offered a degree in educational administration less than 30 minutes from his apartment. Heeding his mother's advice, he decided the degree was not only convenient but satisfied his need to increase his salary. It would also leave him with a new certification just in case he decided to use it. He completed the bulk of his internship experiences right in Whitney, with a principal who was the most recent in a series of administrators rotated through the school over the past ten years. No one expected this man to stay. Rumor had it he was waiting for an opportunity to be principal in one of the larger middle schools in another part of the city. Even so, Nick found him to be a competent administrator who was honest about Whitney's strengths and its weaknesses.

Nick's break came when his principal told him that he would be transferred soon. He was sure central administration would be open to a first-time principal as his replacement, especially someone as knowledgeable about Whitney as Nick. Nick enthusiastically applied for the job. He was certain his positive working relationship with his fellow teachers would result in their enthusiastic support of his candidacy. Nick was somewhat taken aback by the tough grilling the interview committee of teachers and parents gave him. It became clear to him that the interview committee, carefully appointed by central office so that it represented all local and administrative perspectives, was experiencing internal conflict. The committee members did not seem to share one view of what they wanted in a principal. Some even seemed to doubt his sincerity when he said he believed in meeting the needs of all of Whitney's students. Couldn't they tell he loved Whitney and only wanted to serve Whitney's children? Didn't they know he respected Whitney's historic dedication to the community?

Nick got the job, but his ego was bruised in the process. Everyone looked at him differently now, and he found himself looking at his teaching colleagues differently, as well. A teacher whose high standards and effective, though traditional, teaching methods Nick formerly respected now became a barrier to change. Nick began to see other teachers he once admired for aggressively procuring resources for their classrooms as narrowly pursuing personal agendas, not as team players dedicated to serving the entire school population.

Nick's family was proud of him for landing his first principalship just after his 29th birthday. Even as he beamed at the party his parents and fiancée held for him, he began to panic. What if he wasn't ready? How could he get a handle on himself and the school?

Nick began by checking himself on some basic skills. Nick decided to be highly critical as he sorted through the standards proposed by the National Policy Board on Educational Administration. Nick felt it was very important to identify areas where he justifiably had a great deal of confidence as well as areas in which he needed help.

WORKSHEET FOR SELF-ANALYSIS ON PRINCIPALSHIP KNOWLEDGE AND SKILLS

Leadership

1 - - - - - 2 - - - - - ③ - - - - - 4 - - - - - 5
Undeveloped   **Refined**

Issues to Consider: I have a well-developed educational philosophy I share with others. I can get groups of people to agree and to accomplish important tasks. I am a good role model; my actions are those of a good educator and others try to be like me. I visualize the future and strategize ways to move my school toward that future.

Information Collection

1 - - - - - ②- - - - - 3 - - - - - 4 - - - - - 5
Undeveloped   **Refined**

Issues to Consider: I seek tangible and relevant data before making important decisions. I investigate a variety of sources before making important decisions. I use technology to collect and process information.

Problem Analysis

1 - - - - - ②- - - - - 3 - - - - - 4 - - - - - 5
Undeveloped   **Refined**

Issues to Consider: I avoid implementing a solution until I thoroughly understand the problem. I generate more than one hypothesis for the cause of a problem. I generate more than one possible and workable solution.

Judgment

1 - - - - (2-) - - - - 3 - - - - - 4 - - - - - 5
Undeveloped   **Refined**

Issues to Consider: I effectively forecast whether something will be a real problem. I discriminate between information that is reliable, of high quality, and of importance from that which is misleading, false, or inconsequential. I reach conclusions based on logic. I store and recall information at a level sufficient to make effective decisions.

Organizational Oversight

1 - - - - (2-) - - - - 3 - - - - - 4 - - - - - 5
Undeveloped   **Refined**

Issues to Consider: I work with others to develop and implement short- and long-range plans. I abandon work that distracts from the goals of the organization. I understand and use several strategies for managing and monitoring multiple long-range projects.

Implementation

1 - - - - - 2 - - - - (3 -) - - - - 4 - - - - - 5
Undeveloped   **Refined**

Issues to Consider: I make things happen and others want to participate. I understand and use various approaches to organizational change. I believe that midcourse corrections are sometimes necessary and desirable.

Delegation

1 - - - - (2-) - - - - 3 - - - - - 4 - - - - - 5
Undeveloped   **Refined**

Issues to Consider: I allow and expect others to be part of the decision-making and action-taking team. I am clear about my expectations regarding the authority and responsibility others in the organization have for acceptably completing tasks.

Instructional Program

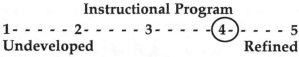

1- - - - - 2- - - - - 3- - - - - -(4-)- - - - 5
Undeveloped   Refined

Issues to Consider: I recognize that children's learning needs differ. I make decisions based on how their consequences will affect student learning. I involve professionals, support staff, and parents in creating a positive learning environment for students.

Curriculum Design

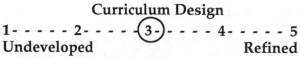

1- - - - - 2- - - - -(3-)- - - - 4- - - - - 5
Undeveloped   Refined

Issues to Consider: I work with others to align curriculum and assessment across grade levels. I work with others to constantly monitor social and technological developments for ways they might affect the curriculum.

Student Guidance and Development

1- - - - - 2- - - - -(3-)- - - - 4- - - - - 5
Undeveloped   Refined

Issues to Consider: I believe the school should find ways to provide guidance, counseling, and auxiliary services to students. I work with others to find ways to connect schooling with plans for adult life. I work with others to link school-sponsored activities with learning.

Staff Development

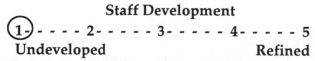

(1-)- - - - 2- - - - - 3- - - - - 4- - - - - 5
Undeveloped   Refined

Issues to Consider: I have experience assessing development needs of teachers and other staff. I have experience designing and implementing learning experiences for adults. I know how to align individual development needs and organizational needs to create effective and efficient staff development programs.

Measurement and Evaluation

1- - - - - 2- - - - -(3-)- - - - 4- - - - - 5
Undeveloped   Refined

Issues to Consider: I gather and use appropriate data to determine needs of students, staff, and the school. I work with others to establish standards, to measure progress toward meeting standards, and to revise instructional programs appropriately.

Resource Allocation

(1)- - - - 2- - - - - 3- - - - - 4- - - - - 5
Undeveloped   Refined

Issues to Consider: I work with others to develop realistic budgets. I find ways to balance the budget despite changing conditions throughout the year. I work with others to find ways to share resources.

Motivating Others

1- - - - - 2- - - - - 3- - - - (4-)- - - - 5
Undeveloped   Refined

Issues to Consider: I can get others to build a commitment to a course of action. I recognize and reward the performance of others. I support and reinforce appropriate innovations.

Sensitivity

1- - - - - 2- - - - - 3- - - - (4-)- - - - 5
Undeveloped   Refined

Issues to Consider: I perceive the needs and concerns of others quickly. I am tactful. I work with others in emotionally stressful situations to reduce conflicts. I adapt my approach to my audiences.

Oral Expression

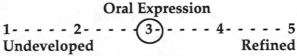

1- - - - - 2- - - - (3-)- - - - 4- - - - - 5
Undeveloped   Refined

Issues to Consider: I make clear and easy-to-understand presentations. I ask clarifying questions. I summarize on behalf of the group. I listen as well as I talk.

Written Expression

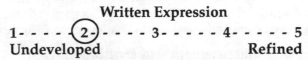

1- - - - (2-)- - - - 3- - - - - 4- - - - - 5
Undeveloped   Refined

Issues to Consider: I express ideas clearly in writing. I write appropriately for different audiences. I can prepare concise but considerate memoranda.

Philosophical and Cultural Values

1 - - - - - 2 - - - - - 3 - - - - - (4) - - - - - 5

Undeveloped   **Refined**

Issues to Consider: I recognize philosophical and historical influences on education. I understand the reciprocal influences of education and culture. I have a well-defined personal philosophy of the role of education in society. I operate within a well-defined ethical system.

Legal and Regulatory Applications

1 - - - - - (2) - - - - - 3 - - - - - 4 - - - - - 5

Undeveloped   **Refined**

Issues to Consider: I act according to laws, rules, and policies relevant to schools. I recognize governmental influences on education. I understand how to administer contracts. I use a reliable resource to remain current regarding important court decisions that affect building-level decisions.

Policy and Political Influences

1 - - - - (2) - - - - - 3 - - - - - 4 - - - - - 5

Undeveloped   **Refined**

Issues to Consider: I identify public policy issues that affect education. I work through professional and public groups to promote policies related to student welfare.

Public and Media Relationships

(1) - - - - 2 - - - - - 3 - - - - - 4 - - - - - 5

Undeveloped   **Refined**

Issues to Consider: I work with media to develop informed perceptions about school issues. I interact effectively with parental and community opinion leaders. I respond skillfully to electronic and printed news media. I initiate news reports about my school.

SELF-REFLECTION ON THE PRINCIPALSHIP: INTRODUCING ELIZABETH HARRIS

As the smallest of four public high schools in a community of approximately 100,000, Central High School serves 600 students in grades 9–12. The community grew slowly over the

years through tenuous cooperation between well-landed farm-
ers and white-collar employees of a large insurance company,
two hospitals with nursing schools, and two expanding colleges. Seven years ago a modern automated automobile plant
opened at the edge of town, locating 200 new employees and
their families in the community, primarily in neighborhoods
served by Central High School. Although Central hired six
new faculty in the past two years, most of the 48 faculty and
12 support staff have been with Central for more than a decade.
Loyalty to Central is so strong in the community that seven of
the teachers and two of the support staff attended Central as
students.

Forty-year-old Elizabeth Harris spent two years as principal of an alternative high school before coming to Central. The
contrast between the two schools was enormous. The alternative school served students who could no longer attend their
home buildings. Many were from poor families. Central served
students from various socioeconomic backgrounds, but most
were from upper- and middle-class families. The alternative
school relied in part on funding by state grants. Central was
well-funded by local tax dollars supplemented by occasional
grants for technology and other innovations. The first line of
responsibility for the alternative school principal was creating
and maintaining an orderly environment. The first line of responsibility for Central's principal was creating a high-achieving environment. The alternative school had been an excellent
test of her integrity and backbone. Elizabeth came to Central
eager to lead a "real" school with "normal" students. She had
proven she was tough enough. Now she wanted to use her
background in curriculum to work as an instructional leader.

Elizabeth's first year at Central didn't measure up to her expectations. Everything seemed to be an emergency. Despite
several attempts to act rather than react, Elizabeth felt no more
on top of things at this "normal" school after one year than she
had at the alternative school She found herself confronted
daily with a legacy of hard feelings created by the paternalistic
principal of ten years who proeceded her. Every time she
thought she had a schedule that she could live with, the central
office, a counselor, or even her secretary would remind her of a
deadline she didn't even know existed.

Elizabeth wanted to be accessible and so maintained an open door policy, reserving early mornings and late evenings for mail and other paperwork. Even so, she found herself frustrated by some of the reasons people dropped in, including parents who seemed to want her to strictly enforce rules except when it came to their children. Their children were either exceptions to rules or were seeking technical loopholes regardless of their personal actions. Teachers seemed to take the same attitude regarding themselves versus other adults in the building. Elizabeth's attempts to cheerlead team spirit drowned in a sea of individuals seeking personal attention and recognition.

At the end of that first year, Elizabeth decided that she would approach her second year more systematically and thoughtfully than she had her first. Determined to be a less reactionary and more effective principal, Elizabeth began her self-directed professional development by completing the worksheet that you and Nick Freeman filled out.

Elizabeth loved Central High School after being there just a year. Like many others, she had been infected by the feeling around Central that anyone associated with the school was a winner. Something in the air exuded confidence and optimism, especially when it came to students. Central's aura of success was inescapable. Even so, Elizabeth knew that not all was well at Central. Under the facade of wellness, a crisis of faith threatened Central's confidence. Elizabeth sensed that teachers and staff, in particular, were holding on to the vestiges of past glory even as they took private precautions against changing times and an uncertain future.

Elizabeth decided she must find ways to make the feelings about Central's past, present, and future tangible to herself and to the others who worked so hard at the school. She began by thinking about her ability to perform in these 21 knowledge and skill domains. Elizabeth tried to be honest with herself and critical of her skills. Results of her analysis are summarized on the following pages.

WORKSHEET FOR SELF-ANALYSIS ON PRINCIPALSHIP KNOWLEDGE AND SKILLS

Leadership

1 - - - - - 2 - - - - - ③ - - - - - 4 - - - - - 5
Undeveloped   Refined

Issues to Consider: I have a well-developed educational philosophy I share with others. I can get groups of people to agree and to accomplish important tasks. I am a good role model; my actions are those of a good educator and others try to be like me. I visualize the future and strategize ways to move my school toward that future.

Information Collection

1 - - - - ②- - - - - 3 - - - - - 4 - - - - - 5
Undeveloped   Refined

Issues to Consider: I seek tangible and relevant data before making important decisions. I investigate a variety of sources before making important decisions. I use technology to collect and process information.

Problem Analysis

1 - - - - ②- - - - - 3 - - - - - 4 - - - - - 5
Undeveloped   Refined

Issues to Consider: I avoid implementing a solution until I thoroughly understand the problem. I generate more than one hypothesis for the cause of a problem. I generate more than one possible and workable solution.

Judgment

1 - - - - ②- - - - 3 - - - - - 4 - - - - - 5
Undeveloped   Refined

Issues to Consider: I effectively forecast whether something will be a real problem. I discriminate between information that is reliable, of high quality, and of importance from that which is misleading, false, or inconsequential. I reach conclusions based on logic. I store and recall information at a level sufficient to make effective decisions.

Organizational Oversight

1 - - - - (2-) - - - - 3 - - - - - 4 - - - - - 5
Undeveloped   Refined

Issues to Consider: I work with others to develop and implement short- and long-range plans. I abandon work that distracts from the goals of the organization. I understand and use several strategies for managing and monitoring multiple long-range projects.

Implementation

1 - - - - - 2 - - - - (3-) - - - - 4 - - - - - 5
Undeveloped   Refined

Issues to Consider: I make things happen and others want to participate. I understand and use various approaches to organizational change. I believe that midcourse corrections are sometimes necessary and desirable.

Delegation

1 - - - - (2-) - - - - 3 - - - - - 4 - - - - - 5
Undeveloped   Refined

Issues to Consider: I allow and expect others to be part of the decision-making and action-taking team. I am clear about my expectations regarding the authority and responsibility others in the organization have for acceptably completing tasks.

Instructional Program

1 - - - - - 2 - - - - - 3 - - - - (4-) - - - - 5
Undeveloped   Refined

Issues to Consider: I recognize that children's learning needs differ. I make decisions based on how their consequences will affect student learning. I involve professionals, support staff, and parents in creating a positive learning environment for students.

Curriculum Design

1 - - - - - 2 - - - - (3-) - - - - 4 - - - - - 5
Undeveloped   Refined

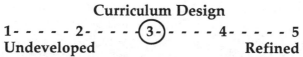

Issues to Consider: I work with others to align curriculum and assessment across grade levels. I work with others to constantly monitor social and technological developments for ways they might affect the curriculum.

Student Guidance and Development

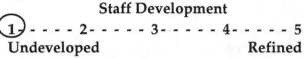

1 - - - - - 2 - - - - - (3 -) - - - - 4 - - - - - 5
Undeveloped   Refined

Issues to Consider: I believe the school should find ways to provide guidance, counseling and auxiliary services to students. I work with others to find ways to connect schooling with plans for adult life. I work with others to link school-sponsored activities with learning.

Staff Development

(1) - - - - 2 - - - - - 3 - - - - - 4 - - - - - 5
Undeveloped   Refined

Issues to Consider: I have experience assessing development needs of teachers and other staff. I have experience designing and implementing learning experiences for adults. I know how to align individual development needs and organizational needs to create effective and efficient staff development programs.

Measurement and Evaluation

1 - - - - - 2 - - - - (3 -) - - - - 4 - - - - - 5
Undeveloped   Refined

Issues to Consider: I gather and use appropriate data to determine needs of students, staff, and the school. I work with others to establish standards, to measure progress toward meeting standards, and to revise instructional programs appropriately.

Resource Allocation

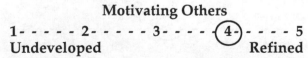

(1 -) - - - - 2 - - - - - 3 - - - - - 4 - - - - - 5
Undeveloped   Refined

Issues to Consider: I work with others to develop realistic budgets. I find ways to balance the budget despite changing conditions throughout the year. I work with others to find ways to share resources.

Motivating Others

1 - - - - - 2 - - - - - 3 - - - - (4 -) - - - - 5
Undeveloped   Refined

Issues to Consider: I can get others to build a commitment to a course of action. I recognize and reward the performance of others. I support and reinforce appropriate innovations.

Sensitivity

1 - - - - - 2 - - - - - 3 - - - - -④- - - - 5
Undeveloped   Refined

Issues to Consider: I perceive the needs and concerns of others quickly. I am tactful. I work with others in emotionally stressful situations to reduce conflicts. I adapt my approach to my audiences.

Oral Expression

1 - - - - - 2 - - - - -③- - - - - 4 - - - - - 5
Undeveloped   Refined

Issues to Consider: I make clear and easy-to-understand presentations. I ask clarifying questions. I summarize on behalf of the group. I listen as well as I talk.

Written Expression

1 - - - - ②- - - - - 3 - - - - - 4 - - - - - 5
Undeveloped   Refined

Issues to Consider: I express ideas clearly in writing. I write appropriately for different audiences. I can prepare concise but considerate memoranda.

Philosophical and Cultural Values

1 - - - - - 2 - - - - - 3 - - - - -④- - - - 5
Undeveloped   Refined

Issues to Consider: I recognize philosophical and historical influences on education. I understand the reciprocal influences of education and culture. I have a well-defined personal philosophy of the role of education in society. I operate within a well-defined ethical system.

Legal and Regulatory Applications

1 - - - - ②- - - - - 3 - - - - - 4 - - - - - 5
Undeveloped   Refined

Issues to Consider: I act according to laws, rules, and policies relevant to schools. I recognize governmental influences on education. I understand how to administer contracts. I use a reliable resource to remain current regarding important court decisions that affect building-level decisions.

Policy and Political Influences

1- - - - (2-) - - - - 3- - - - - 4- - - - - 5
Undeveloped   **Refined**

Issues to Consider: I identify public policy issues that affect education. I work through professional and public groups to promote policies related to student welfare.

Public and Media Relationships

(1-) - - - - 2- - - - - 3- - - - - 4- - - - - 5
Undeveloped   **Refined**

Issues to Consider: I work with media to develop informed perceptions about school issues. I interact effectively with parental and community opinion leaders. I respond skillfully to electronic and printed news media. I initiate news reports about my school.

Overall, Elizabeth saw herself as average to above-average in these 21 knowledge and skills areas. She reviewed the worksheet several times, trying to justify changing some of her self-evaluations, but honesty kept her from changing those she hated to face. She felt good about her abilities in the programmatic domains, especially those associated with curriculum and instruction that are not always strengths for high school principals. Elizabeth also prided herself on her human relations skills and her ability to learn quickly.

At the same time, Elizabeth evaluated herself as poorly executing skills she believed Central really needed in its new principal. Elizabeth realized that she needed to develop new strategies for dealing with Central's future. She needed to serve as a better role model and act concretely to move Central to the future. She vowed to engage herself and the school in the collection and use of data for making decisions, minimizing the influence of emotions and traditions. She needed to exercise stronger organizational oversight and implementation of new directions.

Elizabeth realized that stronger organizational oversight would not mean more autocratic leadership from the principal. She truly believed that organizational oversight meant being better able to trust others, facilitate decisions, and delegate authority. She needed to create an organization that could think and learn. Central's faculty and staff were going to be expected to engage in honest reflection about the purpose of Central High School and their roles in fulfilling that purpose.

Elizabeth's experience of self-reflection was a positive one. It helped her focus on areas of strength and areas for growth. We hope that this first step in self-reflection was equally helpful to you.

2

REFLECTIVE LEADERSHIP

During the 1980s, an extensive body of literature developed from attempts to describe activities that characterized principals of effective schools as instructional leaders. One difficulty with this approach is that there are many different kinds of school settings, and the range of ways in which leadership can be exercised is virtually limitless. A related problem is that it is difficult to detect which activities are leadership activities and which are not. Several researchers of that decade tried to identify characteristics shared by effective school leaders.

At least as important as what principals do, but much less well-researched, is what principals think. We know from economics, for example, how important expectations and beliefs are in their impact. The belief that prices must inevitably rise, for example, lay behind the double-digit inflation that plagued the United States during the 1970s as consumers and producers behaved according to their beliefs. Almost a half century earlier, Franklin Roosevelt underscored the importance of beliefs on action when he noted in his first inaugural address that "the only thing we have to fear is fear itself." Norman Vincent Peale was an early advocate of the "power of positive thinking." It should, therefore, come as little surprise that behavioral scientists have at last recognized that thoughts, beliefs, and expectations are legitimate targets for inquiry because they have such predictive power in relationship to the way people will behave.

Much of the literature on school leadership is normative and superficial. It tells principals how they should behave, but fails to provide an account of real behaviors or the reasons principals behave as they do (Ianni, 1979). Descriptions of principals' behaviors without analysis of the reasons for these behaviors ignores the differences in thought processes evidenced by effective and less effective principals (Leithwood, 1987).

An unusual study by the University of Illinois' National Center for School Leadership attempted to expand the definition of school leadership beyond a set of behaviors. Eighty-one principals, their teachers, and their students completed instruments designed to provide data regarding the leader's effectiveness. Following administration of the instruments, each principal was equipped with a radio paging receiver and randomly beeped five times daily for five working days. Each time they received a beep, the principals recorded not only what they were doing, but also their interpretations of the activities and their feelings at the time. The study revealed that principals' beliefs about what they were doing were much more significant than the activities themselves in explaining the differences in leadership effectiveness. Effective and less effective principals engaged in essentially the same activities, but the more effective principals conceptualized and used the activities as opportunities for leadership (Scott, Krug, & Ahadi, 1990).

Principals today engage in a role filled with paradoxes. On the one hand, they must sustain the organization. This means that the principal is responsible for stabilizing the work environment and ensuring that daily operations are predictable and responsible. On the other hand, principals are responsible for leading change. Quinn asserts that effective leaders of organizations reconcile this paradox through a cognitive map of competing values and frameworks. Quinn validates the results of the "beeper" study of principals when he reports that effective leaders think differently than do less effective leaders. They are able to shift their actions from highly directive to team-oriented as the need arises. They do not operate from a single theoretical model (Quinn, 1988).

One of the most perplexing paradoxes faced by principals is that created by the more recent emphasis on shared decision making in the building, which is sometimes called site-based management. It seems to some that the principal's authority has eroded even as school-level accountability has increased. At the same time, principals have not been relieved of their traditional responsibilities. In fact, management responsibilities, such as public relations, facilities management, budgeting, personnel selection, and program evaluation have increased. Principals have become facilitative middle managers, caught between site pressures, central office, and external state mandates (see Hallinger & Hausman, 1994). Effective leaders behave in seemingly paradoxical ways because they see the entire organization and recognize the need to create steady daily operations while moving the organization forward.

According to Murphy (1992), the greatest challenge for school administrators is to lead the school's transition from a bureaucracy to a postindustrial model with the goal of educating all students. Murphy outlines four roles for modern principals:

- administrator as servant leader (shares responsibility, works with people, bases empowerment on democratic principles);
- administrator as organizational architect (focusing on change instead of stability, builds heterarchies instead of hierarchies);
- administrator as social architect (invents ways for schools to adapt to needs of children rather than forcing children to adapt to needs of schools); and
- administrator as moral educator (bases purpose and actions on values and beliefs).

Making this transition requires the ability to call on a range of theoretical bases from which to lead.

A great deal of talk about leadership ultimately defines that term in very specific and restrictive ways. Leaders are carefully distinguished, for example, from supervisors, administrators, managers, and, worst of all, bureaucrats. This kind of thinking leads some people to despair of ever effectively playing a leadership role because they just don't have what it takes. They feel they lack the bravado, boldness, and charisma that seem to be a prerequisite for the job.

If we have learned one thing about effective leaders, it is that they come in all sizes and shapes. What appears to distinguish them from others isn't a distinctive set of characteristics but a distinctive approach that emerges from their personal conceptualization of the task. Effective leaders find diverse, creative ways to accomplish the basic leadership tasks in the ways they interact with teachers, students, parents, and others. These ways are compatible with individual personalities and the contexts in which they operate. In short, effective instructional leaders don't do different things than ineffective leaders;

they do things differently. For example, they seize the opportunity at discipline sessions to remind students not just of the rules, but of the reasons for the rules.

This rather egalitarian view assumes that everyone can be an effective leader of instruction and contribute to the reformation of our schools. In the same way that different composers approach each new work by varying the order and tempo at which they present the same 12 tones, instructional leaders approach the same activities with a different repertoire of motives, experiences, and talents. In both cases the resulting compositions are most likely to be different, but no less enjoyable or potentially effective.

WHAT DO EFFECTIVE PRINCIPALS DO?

We know that if principals fail to meet the various rules and regulations prescribed by state laws, they can be stripped of their administrative certificates and lose their positions. Conversely, we know that if they do perform their administrative duties they will at least keep their certificates and probably their jobs. We know the long list of leadership dimensions and associated skills thoughtfully developed through the National Policy Board. In short, we know something about the kinds of behaviors that describe an administrator, perhaps even a good administrator. But how can we operationally describe what an effective principal does?

What communalities can be found in the activities and style of strategic school leaders? As mentioned earlier, during the decade of the 1980s, an extensive literature developed that attempted to describe the activities that characterized principals of effective schools. One of the difficulties with this literature is that there are many different kinds of school settings, and the range of activities within them is virtually limitless. A related problem is that it is difficult to detect which activities are leadership activities and which are not.

Researchers at the National Center for School Leadership (NCSL) studied this problem in depth. They conducted a series of interlocking studies over nearly a decade that had as their primary focus the identification and measurement of core elements of school leadership. In the same way that physicists had earlier probed the structure of matter to identify basic atomic elements and subelements that transcended specific substances, NCSL researchers looked for an underlying structure that could explain the cohesiveness that was evident across many diverse activities in the behavior of effective principals. The framework they used built on the work of others who sought to understand principals throughout the 1980s, when the term "instructional leadership" came into general use (see, for example, Blasé, 1987; Dwyer, 1985; Eberts & Stone, 1988; Hallinger, 1984; Hallinger & Murphy, 1985; Murphy & Hallinger, 1987; Krug, 1989; Manasse, 1984; Martin & Willower, 1981; Rutherford et al., 1983).

NCSL research ultimately focused on the study of five aspects of the principal's role. Like Lon Chaney, these five themes appeared in many different costumes, but underneath superficial costume differences the actor was the same. Briefly stated, the five core elements were:

- defining and communicating a school's educational mission;
- coordinating curriculum;
- supervising and supporting teaching;
- monitoring student progress; and
- nurturing a positive learning climate.

These five themes became the basis of the development of instruments for studying principal leadership, school climate, and motivation of teachers and principals. The instruments developed by the NCSL are widely used as tools for school improvement (Braskamp & Maehr, 1985; Braskamp & Maehr, 1988a; Braskamp & Maehr, 1988b; Maehr & Ames, 1988; Maehr et al., 1988).

One of the key elements of strategy is prioritization. A strategic leader must be able to prioritize problems, options, and solutions. We believe this "five-factor model" of leadership is particularly important because it provides leaders with a structure for organizing and prioritizing their activities. As successive chapters unfold, we will use these five factors as an organizing structure for leadership development. For that reason, a clear understanding of each is essential to the story we are trying to tell.

DEFINING MISSION

Organizations that do not fully understand why they exist are subject to all sorts of internal and external pressures. A school that has not fully considered how it will go about the process of education has no criteria for judging whether or not a new program is worth pursuing, whether existing programs are living up to their potential, or whether teachers and staff are contributing most effectively.

It isn't possible to overestimate the importance of mission, particularly during a time when schools are being called upon to undergo fundamental structural changes. It is during times of change and transition that a clear sense of purpose becomes even more crucial. Change is usually frightening. Most of us are creatures of habit. We journey cautiously into the unknown. Mission serves to guide that journey, to let us know when we are on track and when we have reached our destination. Operating without a clear mission is like beginning a journey without having a destination—if you don't know where you're going, you probably won't know if or when you get there.

MANAGING CURRICULUM AND INSTRUCTION

The primary service that schools offer is instruction. Effective leaders provide information instructors need to plan, and they actively support curriculum development. Although they do not usually teach, principals need to be aware of the special needs of each instructional area. In science, for example, they need to recognize the importance, and cost, of activity-based instruction. Similarly, in reading, principals need to be aware of newly emerging conceptions of the reading process that argue for an instructional approach that integrates skill acquisition within a focus on broad, integrated strategies. Without this kind of knowledge, principals can neither make judgments about the wisdom of teaching strategies nor provide the resources teachers and staff need to carry out the school's mission effectively.

SUPERVISING AND SUPPORTING TEACHING

The people who most directly fulfill the school's mission are teachers. Partly because of mandates and partly because of traditional hierarchical structuring of administrator-staff relations, principals have usually been assigned an evaluative role with respect to teachers. The focus of the effective instructional leader is more broadly oriented to staff development than to performance evaluation. That is, the effective leader is prospective rather than retrospective regarding faculty and staff. The principal should focus on what can be, not what was. Supervising instruction involves much more than casual classroom visits or annual written evaluations. Supervising instruction involves responsibility for what goes on in the classroom, from hiring, to developing, to using the wisdom of teachers.

MONITORING STUDENT PROGRESS

The school's primary product is a population of graduates who have the intellectual and life skills necessary to cope in an increasingly competitive world. In our society the ultimate test occurs in the marketplace. However, principals provide the first-level quality control check to ensure that this happens. Effective principals need to be aware of the variety of ways in which student progress can and should be assessed. They need to be aware, for example, of both the strengths and limitations of standardized multiple choice tests and of alternative assessment formats. Even more importantly, they need to use assessment results in ways that help teachers and students improve, and parents understand where and why improvement is needed. Monitoring student progress involves understanding of data analysis, curriculum alignment, and student assessment.

Administrators probably feel the greatest level of discomfort in this area because they face technical issues for which their schooling ill prepared them. At the same time, calls for increased accountability have resulted in systems where parents and the general public have extended access to test results. Numbers can be frightening, particularly when we're not comfortable with exactly what they mean or how they are to be interpreted. As they begin to figure more prominently in the school regulation, recognition, and accountability processes, administrators will need to achieve a much higher level of comfort with those kinds of numbers.

PROMOTING INSTRUCTIONAL CLIMATE

When they are first promoted to a management position, some people mistakenly believe that their primary objective is to tell other people what to do. Those who survive for very long in management soon learn that their real objective is to get people to do what needs to be done by creating the conditions under which people want to do it. When the atmosphere of a school is one that makes learning exciting, when teachers and students are supported for their achievements, and when there is a shared sense of purpose, it is difficult not to learn, particularly in the critical first years of school when lifelong attitudes toward education are being formed. One of the definitions of school presented in *Webster's New World Dictionary* (1988) is "a group of persons under some common influence or sharing a unifying belief." School leaders play a critical role in unifying the varied belief systems of teachers, students, and parents. Leaders provide that unifying influence and create schools out of classroom buildings.

Promoting instructional climate is particularly important because it introduces the vehicle by which leadership affects students. It is still true that most students spend little time in the principal's office. Principals are spending less time there, too. Principal-student interactions represent a relatively small proportion of school experiences for most students. So how does the principal's leadership translate into student learning?

Although students may not spend much one-on-one time with the principal, they are continually immersed in the climate and culture of the school. They can no more escape it than they can escape the air that surrounds them. Like air that can be healthy or toxic, the climate of a school can be motivating or discouraging, positive or negative, beneficial or harmful. Many researchers, staff developers, and principals consider climate to be the primary vehicle through which leaders have a pervasive impact on student learning. For example, by communicating a clear mission, principals set certain expectations or norms for learning in the minds of teachers, students, and parents. By providing support for curriculum development, principals allow teachers and students to realize those expectations. In their support of teaching staff, principals increase the personal investment or commitment of teachers. Expectations, norms, possibilities, and beliefs are the elements out of which the cultural fabric of the school is woven.

MORE THAN ABSTRACTIONS

The five dimensions we describe here are more than just abstractions. They have tangible relationships to external criteria by which we judge the success or failure of our schools. The pager study of principals traced a link between those thoughts and the measured achievement levels of their students (Scott, Krug, & Ahadi, 1990). For each school in the study, achievement results on standardized tests of reading and mathematics were available for third, sixth, and eighth grade students. Then, measures of leadership effectiveness of 56 principals at the third grade, 41 principals at sixth grade, and 15 principals at eighth grade were correlated with average achievement test results of their students. The relationship between leadership and student achievement was consistently positive at all three grades. That is, as leadership scores rose, student achievement scores rose; as leadership scores fell, student achievement scores also fell. Across curriculum areas and grades, "Supervising Teaching" showed the highest correlations with student learning, followed closely by "Defining Mission." Predictability was highest at third grade. This seems only reasonable. As students progress in school, learning gains themselves become the best predictors of later success.

ENGAGING IN A PRIVATE DIALOGUE: DEVELOPING A CAREER MAP

We introduced these five dimensions because we believe they offer a practical framework for focusing self-development activities. The next five chapters will turn to each one in much more detail, helping you to reflect upon the link between your behaviors, desired behaviors, and the ideas expressed by these frameworks. However, before we begin the transformation process, you need to get a good idea of where you're starting. It is true that a journey of many miles begins with a single step, and you may be tempted to turn to the next chapter to begin. However, it is equally true that you can't get anywhere unless you know where you're starting.

Unfortunately, fulfilling your need to renew professionally by consciously thinking about the principalship frequently takes a back seat to meeting the needs of others. Staying current, maintaining motivation, and fighting burnout are major challenges for principals, whose midcareer band is broad, lasting as long as 20 or more years (Krupp, 1983; Schein, 1978). Principals need to find ways to reexamine their assumptions and behaviors. As adult learners, principals need to be personally invested in their own development. Sun Yat-sen wrote, "in the construction of a country it is not the practical workers but the idealists and planners that are difficult to find." Principals are the lead idealists and planners in their schools. As such, you owe it to yourself to set aside time to reflect on your role and the work you do.

THINKING REFLECTIVELY

To become a principal who, despite unanticipated interruptions, actively promotes and supports a vision of successful schooling, you must think reflectively. To think reflectively is to study and meditate upon your work. Thinking reflectively requires you to abandon your ego as you engage yourself in a private dialogue about your professional motives and behaviors. Thinking reflectively allows you to direct your professional development as you identify and wrestle with your problems of practice. Just as you want students to use their current talents as foundations for future learning, so you can use your current leadership talents as a solid base for additional learning about leadership. Reflection takes many forms. Keeping a diary is one means of reflection. Another is exchanging letters with a colleague. Some principals share their reflections in articles for newsletters and professional journals. Reflection may also occur in small group settings such as support groups, graduate seminars, or book study groups. A popular approach to reflection is the use of questionnaires such as those appearing in professional periodicals. Readers complete these questionnaires and then check their answers against a scale or set of answers created by the authors.

CREATING A CAREER MAP

Another way to think about where you are is to examine where you have been. In workshops we have conducted with principals, one of the techniques we have found most useful is to have participants create a "career map." A career map creates a visual representation of the forces that have influenced your approach to leadership.

You don't need survey equipment or Rand McNally experts to help you build a career map. All you need is a piece of paper, a pencil, and the following instructions. Begin at a point that makes sense to you. For some, it might be the point at which they realized they wanted to be a teacher. For others, the starting point might be their sophomore year in college when they changed majors. Others might start with their first job. From the starting point, use straight, slanted, and curved lines to depict the path from one career move to the next. Some people draw cul-de-sacs along the road to indicate paths taken that led right back to the point of departure. Dead-end roads off the main path indicate options that were tried but that did not work. Use common road signs to indicate times of challenges (road under construction?) and times of fast progress (interstate highway?). Consider adding notes and symbols to indicate times that your personal and professional lives affected each other. Highlight shifts that changed the ways you thought about yourself or your profession.

The primary purpose of drawing your career map is to provide a visual representation of your career. What opportunities took you down new paths? What choices did you strategically pursue? Did you follow interests that were fulfilling but created indirect routes to your present position? What role did education, personal relationships, and mentors play? The act of drawing your career map will cause you to reflect on your opportunities and decisions and think about the decisions you will make in the future. It will also help you understand and be able to explain experiences that have caused you to think, believe, and behave as you do in your current role.

The map may be linear or it may take other shapes. It may have dips, circles, hubs with arms, and cul-de-sacs. It may spiral back on itself. It may have breaks. Be sure to create a legend. Some signs you might consider using include: Stop, Yield, School Zone, Construction, Red Light, Yellow Light, Green Light, Cul-de-sac, Dead End, Not a Through Road, Construction Zone, Interstate Highway, Two-Lane Road, One Way, Interstate Ends, Intersection.

Don't be in a hurry. Draw your career map when you will not be interrupted or rushed. Then put it away for a few hours or days. When you return to it, study your map, adjust the roads, and add details. Take a few minutes to jot down how

critical decisions, incidents, and people have affected your beliefs and actions as you teach and lead at your school. Repeat
this process until you have a clear map. After studying the
map, make notes for yourself about the critical turning points
on your map and the experiences that influenced your thinking and values the most.

Use the model of Elizabeth Harris's career map presented
on the next page to design your career map. As Elizabeth did,
be sure to include "signs" that have affected your career opportunities and choices along the way.

ELIZABETH HARRIS: LOOKING FORWARD BY LOOKING BACK

Elizabeth knew that actions speak louder than words. The
best way to communicate the importance of reflection and
learning was to engage in it herself. She began by analyzing her
career path. She needed to analyze the decisions she had made,
the paths she had selected, and the challenges she had met.
Drawing a map of her career would provide visual clues to
what made her tick, to what she valued. She used straight lines,
wavy lines, and road signs to represent easy and difficult moments in her career. She included significant personal incidents
that had shaped her career path. Elizabeth put down the map
several times, returning to it over a period of days before she
was satisfied she had fully depicted her career and important
influences on it.

Elizabeth's map, shown on the next page, revealed a career
path not unlike that of many administrators of this decade. She
had, in some ways, wandered around. Wandering around had
been about exploring interests, acquiring education, developing expertise, gaining confidence, and seeking fit. Her diversions into positions of interest, but not directly leading into the
principalship had, she felt, added to her expertise and caused
her to think about the principalship more broadly, with more
interests in mind, than she might have had had she come to a
public school principalship straight from a classroom. Her will-
ingness to postpone part of her career while her husband completed school and during the birth of their first child underscored the way she and her husband felt about the importance
of family. Her pursuit of degrees, even though it meant long

ELIZABETH'S CAREER MAP

7th Grade

I knew I wanted to be a teacher

Greenlight

College Graduation

7th Grade Teacher (4 years)

Job as TV Commercial Writer

Yield

Road Under Construction

moved so husband could earn masters

Earned Master's in Administration

H.S. Teacher (3 years)

Birth of daughter

Yield

2 year hiatus

H.S. Teacher (2 years)

Greenlight

H.S. Assistant Principal

Alternative School Principal

State Department Consultant

Earned Doctorate

Principal of Central High

hours and family sacrifices, represented the importance of support and of education in her life. After all, the principalship is,
in many ways, a family career.

Elizabeth thought about how her work in the alternative
school had tested her integrity daily. She had become both an
administrator and a realist during that experience. But she had
not lost her hope. The experience as an alternative school
principal had convinced her, more than ever, that the public
schools had an important role to play in helping young people
realize their potentials. She earnestly believed, after working
with those students, that public schools had an obligation to
serve children and their parents; that public schools offered the
best hope for a better world. More than anything, she wanted
to be part of that future by helping to shape those who would
build it.

NICK FREEMAN: SPIRALING INTO A CAREER

Elizabeth's career map revealed numerous diversions and
side trips. In contrast, Nick found his career difficult to translate into a visual at first. Although his decision to become a
teacher was so profound he could not remember wanting to be
something else, his move into administration came much more
quickly than he had dreamed possible.

Nick finally decided to depict his career map (shown on
page 50) as an "unwinding" road. At the risk of making it look
something like the yellow brick road from "The Wizard of Oz,"
Nick began by drawing a large spiral. At the center or "eye" of
the spiral Nick noted the event that brought to the conscious
level the desire to become a teacher. Working with third graders when he was a high school sophomore had introduced him
to the joys of contributing to a child's intellectual and personal
development.

Since that experience, Nick had felt as if he was uncoiling,
expanding on his calling. The second layer of his spiral, expanding his own learning, occurred in college when he combined the love of children and teaching with his love of science.
Graduation was the bridge to the continuing growth of his career spiral, leading to teaching at Whitney. Things slowed a bit
as Nick learned to be a teacher of children and a colleague of
other professionals. Several times his abilities as a teacher and
colleague were challenged. One challenge was the frequent

NICK FREEMAN'S CAREER MAP

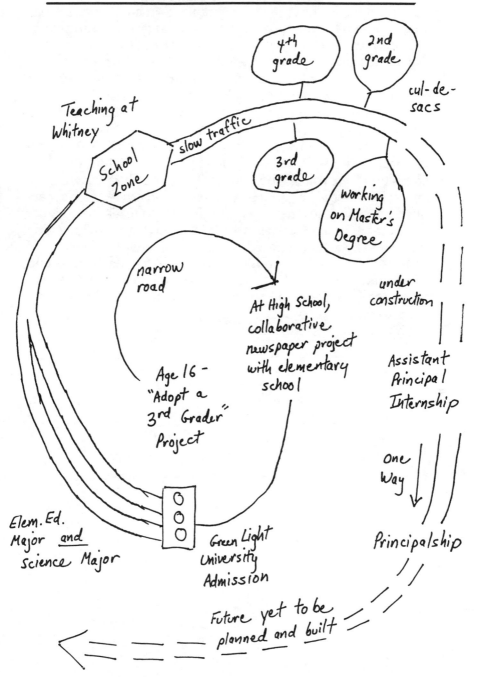

switch to different grade levels. Nick decided to represent these changes within the same organization and profession as cul-de-sacs on his map. An opportunity to serve as administrative intern to the principal became a road under construction as his learning and experience spiral continued to uncoil.

The transfer of his principal to another school, combined with a successful administrative internship, put Nick on a one-way street to the principalship. As Nick reflected on his somewhat "fast track" career at Whitney, he thought about both the opportunities and the barriers facing him. A construction barrier in his career road map indicated for him the challenges he faces as a young principal in a building in which he almost literally grew up. How could he possibly get teachers much his senior, teachers who taught him to teach, to do what he told them to do? Why should they listen to him? What made him think he was prepared for this? How would he get his feelings of uncertainty under control so that he could look and behave like a principal? It was clear to Nick that a great deal of his career was yet to be constructed, including what he was going to do tomorrow.

PART II

A FRAMEWORK FOR LEADERSHIP DEVELOPMENT

Developing a Framework

Lists of knowledge and skills can be found throughout the literature. The framework that forms the core of this book goes beyond simple listings of knowledge and skills. The framework is a useful way of thinking about the artful integration of what you know, can do, and believe into a uniquely effective expertise as a principal. The self-assessment you completed in Part I was based on the NPBEA standards. Its purpose was to help you begin to consciously consider the administrative knowledge and skills you use on a daily basis. You may have come across some skills you almost never use. If you think critically about why those skills seldom come into play, you may have to admit that you don't know how to use them.

Even so, most people with whom you work may not even notice. Perhaps you compensate by being especially skilled in other areas. Maybe someone you can trust makes up for what you lack in a particular area.

These coping mechanisms will get you by, even serve you well, but they prevent you from growing into a school leadership expert. To complete your reflection regarding your competence in the NPBEA standards, you must strategically plan to acquire and practice those skills not currently in your repertoire. Even if you are lucky enough to have someone else who performs some of the tasks associated with a domain, you must keep in mind that the quality of that work is still your responsibility. Much of the knowledge and skill you now use was acquired as your career advanced.

Your career map identified key opportunities for professional growth presented to you in your past. As you strive to become "expert," you must become increasingly self-conscious of creating opportunities to learn more about your chosen profession. Acquiring those skills may be as simple as asking someone to show you how to monitor your practice. Or you may have to participate in a workshop, course, or advanced education.

Each of the next five chapters focuses on one of the five dimensions of leadership we introduced you to in the last chapter. As these chapters unfold, we describe a framework of research-based perspectives, skills, and behaviors practiced by principals of improving schools. We also provide guides to enriching your own approach to the principalship. The five dimensions provide a structure for thinking about the function and role of leadership in schools. Each dimension represents measurable and observable characteristics of schools led by effective principals.

Developing a clear understanding of your personal and professional values is essential to leading others through a journey to a place that even you, the leader, may have never seen. You must be clear about what matters to you as an individual and as a school leader so that no one who works with you mistakes the criteria against which you make decisions. You must be able to express clearly and convincingly, first to yourself and then to others, the principles so essential to you that no mistakes are made about where you draw the line. How far you will go in pursuing the balance of doing good things for children and demonstrating organizational allegiance to your school district's administrative posture must be clear. You must know yourself well enough to select a school that "fits" you and the values you live if you are to sleep well. You must know yourself well enough to know when you can work inside an organization to best serve students. You must also know yourself well enough to know when a fight is worth the ultimate price, your job.

Picture self-knowledge as a microscope with three lenses: personal philosophy, vision, and mission. *Personal philosophy* defines in a few words the values by which someone lives and which they express in their decisions and actions. Personal philosophy reflects one's moral code and gives meaning to life. *Vision* depicts the world as we would like it to be, the world we would like to create. *Mission* intervenes between personal philosophy and vision. Simply put, mission is the action step by which we bridge the gap between the world as it is and the world as we see it in our visions.

PERSONAL PHILOSOPHY

Self-knowledge for principals requires using these three lenses to define what matters, both personally and professionally. Begin by looking through the personal philosophy lens. Your personal philosophy involves values so dear that they guide your life and can never be compromised. These values are so much a part of you that they are obvious in your actions, both at home and at work. What drives you? Take a few minutes to reflect on that question. Choose a few words (25 or less) that make clear your foundational values, words that give expression to your personal philosophy.

This is not an idle exercise. We are reminded by McCall (1994) that, "We don't heed opinions that are contrary to our basic values....Principals who really put children first will run a totally different school than those who give higher priority to other values: their own professional advancement, cutting costs, high ranking on tests, peace at any price, control, popularity with teachers or parents, etc." (p. 31). McCall also reminds us that as spokespeople for their schools, principals communicate what is important while they are at the helm. As principal you are responsible for making sure that people know what you as principal and what your school as an organization stand for.

Now, rotate the lens of personal philosophy just a bit so that it evolves into the lens of educational philosophy. How does what matters most to you personally carry over to your work life? Make no mistake: your personal philosophy shapes your educational philosophy and influences the decisions you make on the job. How do *your* personal values translate to the educational setting? What values or principles lay behind your words and actions when you deal with teachers, students, parents, and others? What pushes your button and really makes you angry? Answering these questions for yourself will lead you to find the words (but not too many words!) to clearly and succinctly share your educational philosophy with others. You began answering this question in earnest for yourself the day you experienced your first "AHA!" education moment. "AHA!" moments, which you experience only rarely, occur when you have insight into just what being an educator is all about. For example, an "AHA!" moment occurs when you receive a letter from a student you thought was destined for jail who thanks you for turning her around with words you don't even remember saying. An "AHA!" moment occurs when you change strategies midstream because you suddenly really know how to teach a particular concept to a particular group of children. An "AHA!" moment occurs when a child kept in from recess reads you a story he couldn't read yesterday or when you discover that a student in danger of being kicked out of your class needs glasses more than he needs discipline. Every educator has "AHA!" moments, moments that alter our educational philosophies.

VISION

Your personal vision represents your dream of how things should be. For example, most parents have a vision of the world in which they want their children to live, and it is better than the one in which they live. Some of us see visions of world peace, interracial harmony, or pollution-free environments. We hold these visions both because they are beautiful dreams just out of our reach and because we believe that through our choices we can move closer to trading the current reality for those dreams. Moreover, if others would just share our dreams and our choice, the dreams just might come true.

Now rotate the lens of personal vision into the lens of educational vision. Your educational vision is the picture drawn in your mind when you imagine the ideal school. You know all about it because you began making it up when you first started your career. Construction continued as you fantasized about the school you would love to start if you could just find the resources. You redesigned it every time you read a journal article about a successful educational setting or strategy you wished you could incorporate into your current practice. Every day you compare the school in which you currently work to your vision of the ideal. The first challenge is finding the right words to describe this ideal school. The next challenge is helping others to see the same vision. Finally, you want to engage others in seeking ways to move the reality of your school closer to the fantasy of the vision. Fantasies may be fantastic, but they are usually not completely out of the realm of possibility. Failure to create an educational vision that you share and mold in collaboration with others involved in your school leaves you subject to the whims of external forces. Roland Barth (1990) makes this point in *Improving Schools from Within* when he writes, "Another good reason for schoolpeople (sic) to formulate and articulate their own visions of the way their schools ought to be is that by *not* doing so, they invite random prescription from outside: from the central office, from the state department of education, from national commissions and task forces. There is already too much random behavior in schools" (p. 152).

Mission

Philosophies are deeply personal and individual, although several of us may be guided by similar philosophies. A vision, although personal, is more easily shared as we can use words and pictures to attract others to our dreams for the future. A principal and staff who share the same vision for their school would list the same characteristics or draw the same picture if they were separately asked about the school. Even as a principal shares and works with others to develop a vision of how the school should be, the school community must also develop a shared means of moving toward realizing the vision. A mission must be shared and agreed upon by the members of the school organization if the school is to change in a rational and planned way. A shared mission makes it likely that we will use finite resources wisely. Competing missions within an organization, even when inspired by the same vision, may result in poor planning, shoddy implementation, redundancy, and wasted resources.

Your mission is dependent on your philosophy and vision. If they are unclear, you wander around without a sense of mission. Before we move on to how great principals use mission, take time to put your values into words.

- ♦ Try to write down your personal philosophy. What guides your life's decisions? Can you put it in a few words that roll easily off your tongue and that others understand easily?

- ♦ Try to put your educational philosophy into a few words (25 or less). Is it so true to your personal philosophy that you can say it without hesitating? Does it make clear the values against which you weigh administrative decisions? Do you *really* weigh decisions against these ideas (if not, you have some pretty words here, but you have not identified your real educational philosophy).

- ♦ Give words to your vision of school. Make a few notes to yourself about your ideal school. What does it look like? Who is there? How do people behave when alone and when in the company of others? How does it feel? What do you do there?

3

DEVELOPING, COMMUNICATING, AND LIVING A SCHOOL MISSION

THE ROLE OF MISSION

What does it mean to be on a mission? If you go on a mission, you undertake a journey with a specific purpose in mind. Mankind's history is replete with examples of missions. We have joined missions to the New World, to the bottom of the sea, to the moon, Mars, and beyond. A mission may be philanthropic, self-serving, peace-seeking, relationship-seeking, or knowledge-seeking. A mission may be goal-focused, clearly complete when an identified task is achieved or a specified destination reached. A mission may also be open-ended, complete only when time, money, or human capacity runs out. Sometimes a mission is complete when those who commit to it realize satisfaction from the process of undertaking the mission, regardless of intended outcomes.

Whatever form it takes, however, a mission is always strategic and purposeful. Missions give human beings reasons to get up every day, to make choices, and to devote their personal and professional energies to chosen organizations, people, and causes. Regardless of the label you choose, having a mission is to have an immediate purpose in life.

This might be a good time to continue the discussion we started earlier and revisit the relationship of "vision" and "mission." A vision reflects some notion of the ideal. To have a vision is to hold deep inside you a picture of what an ideal world would be like. In your vision, you see how the world looks, how people behave, what results from the efforts of people in that world. Mission, on the other hand, is very much rooted in the real world. Your mission is the set of strategies you engage in to realize that vision. Although the vision can be shared, missions can be quite different, often incompatible. For example, a vision of world peace leads some people to engage in relief missions to war-torn countries; others may set out on military campaigns. Still others embark on ambassadorial missions. Some seek this vision closer to home through participation in community service organizations. Mission bridges present reality to an ideal. Because present realities differ from one person to another, despite a shared vision of the ideal, missions take on very different characters.

Below is an example of one person's personal philosophy, vision, and mission statement. This mission statement is a very concrete, action-oriented way of bringing a personal philosophy and vision into reality. You can easily think of many other ways to do so. Many teachers would find the philosophy and vision agreeable but identify missions that are compatible with working in the local classroom.

Personal philosophy: The nature of human beings is to explore and learn. I will live my life exploring and learning from new ideas, places, and people.

Vision: The world will become a peaceful place when people are able to better communicate with each other.

Mission: Join the Peace Corps to work with underdeveloped nations to connect their people to each other and to the world through new communications technology.

Television shows and movies have sometimes done us a disservice by suggesting that missions are either impossible or heroic. Neither characteristic is a defining element of mission. First, a mission must be doable. Our vision may be to teach the world to sing in perfect harmony, but we need to fine-tune that thought into a doable mission that recognizes the existence of tone-deaf people.

Throughout life our personal missions change. They change for many understandable reasons. For starters, as we mature, experience the world, interact with other people, discover spiritual needs, and pursue intellectual challenges, our vision of possibilities for ourselves and our world changes. As this vision changes, so do our strategies for striving to realize our vision. We may experience limited missions when we are young, such as completing each grade of elementary school to satisfy our vision of ourselves as high achievers. We may also spend some time lost in adolescence with no sense of mission and logic to our decisions. As adults, most of us journey on numerous personal and professional missions, fulfilling some and abandoning others.

At its root, a mission serves as the standard against which you make decisions about how to use your precious resources of time, energy, money, intellect, and emotion. If your sense of mission is particularly strong, you may recruit others to join your mission. You may also refuse to engage in certain activities because they detract from or run counter to your mission. For example, a mission to repair the space shuttle requires certain tools. Those undertaking that mission carry the tools necessary to their purpose, but do not spend precious weight and cargo space restrictions on unnecessary paraphernalia, regardless of how interesting or amusing it may be.

People expect businesses to have missions. Certainly the missions of Walmart, Ben and Jerry's Ice Cream, and Mary Kay Cosmetics not only distinguish them from each other, but communicate what they intend to accomplish and how they intend to do so. The differences in their missions account for the different types of decisions each organization makes. No doubt, the mission of each business has altered over the years as customers, market forces, suppliers, and other conditions changed. Just as human beings need a series of missions throughout their lifetimes to give them a continued sense of purpose in which they can emotionally, intellectually, and physically invest, organizations have this need. Having a mission at any given time is important to organizations in part because people make up organizations. It stands to reason that if individuals need purpose, so do organizations, which are made up of people.

A sense of mission is critical for all types of organizations, but especially so for schools, which have the primary responsibility after the family for educating and socializing our children. It is easy for us to take for granted that we know what the mission of a school is because schools are thoroughly woven into the fabric of our society. The market forces, which constantly pressure businesses to confront their fragility, have not historically hammered schools as severely. Most people, at least until the last decade, took schools for granted. Now many take for granted that the schools should be either what they experienced or what they would like to have experienced. Others assume that schools *are* their physical plants, as solid or shaky as the materials of which they are built.

As we said, the mission of schools is too often taken for granted. Usually, the buildings have existed for decades. Each year brings a new crop of students into one end of the building and an old crop out the other. There is seldom a need to recruit the new crop; they just arrive in the normal course of events, with an inevitability like that of the changing seasons. The problem, of course, is that the new crop has new needs. Strategies that worked with their parents are unlikely to work with them. Their information needs are different. Their orientation to the world is different. Lesson plans—and mission—must be reevaluated, refined, and redirected.

Whenever the purpose of the school goes without saying, the school goes nowhere. Excellent principals and their schools are distinguished from others by their consciousness of purpose and dynamic commitment to accomplishing their educational missions. Each school needs a mission that invests the emotional, intellectual, and physical efforts of its people so that everyone knows why it exists, what it values, and how decisions will be made. Without a mission, a school has no standard against which to make important decisions about human and capital resource selection and expenditure. Schools, like people, experience life-altering conditions. Because local communities, state and national governments, and international competitiveness affect schools, their missions may change several times over a half-century. What is important is that the mission is known and shared.

Think of the best school in which you have worked. When asked, could you cite the school's mission? If not, if you had to look it up, the school had no real mission. What about your current school? A mission that is on paper in a notebook on a shelf but not known, embraced, and espoused by nearly everyone associated with the school is a fraud. Real school missions are words given to heartfelt beliefs about what we must accomplish to call ourselves a successful school.

The following are examples of educators' personal philosophies, educational philosophies, educational visions, and school missions.

Example One

Personal philosophy: Doing the right thing is its own reward for those who always strive to do the right thing for students.

Educational philosophy: No action or word goes unnoticed in educational settings. The key to good schools is people working in them and with them who always strive to do the right thing for students. Good role models are the best teachers.

Educational vision: The ideal school exudes the joy of learning. Adults in the school work together to constantly improve their individual and group expertise. Student and adult teams explore learning through a dynamic combination of experiences using all the tools available. The joy of learning becomes a reward in itself, with grades serving only as benchmarks of progress.

School mission: Our school prepares students to use every opportunity to learn, sending them into the world ready not only to work, but to continue learning how to work better.

Example Two

Personal philosophy: Each individual is responsible for his or her behavior. I must account to others and myself for my mistakes as well as for my successes.

Educational philosophy: Schools should teach students the importance of hard work and personal responsibility for their actions.

Educational vision: The ideal school makes clear expectations for students and teachers, holding everyone accountable to high standards. A school should run smoothly. Its routines should be predictable, and every effort should be made to help students succeed academically and personally.

School mission: Our school prepares students to be responsible citizens and productive members of society.

DOING MISSION

Schools must have clear purposes that everyone associated with them shares. Most people nod their heads in agreement with this "mom and apple pie" statement, but secretly dismiss it. Most of those people have probably never baked an apple pie. Selecting the best ingredients, rolling the dough, seasoning the filling, and baking the pie to perfection is a delicate and intricate job. It requires intelligence, dexterity, intuition, and attention to detail. Compromising on the ingredients, spilling too much flour into the dough, or overbaking results in a pie no one will eat. Developing and communicating the mission for which your school lives is no less delicate an operation.

Few school missions result from divine inspiration. Most are born of hard work. This work includes knowing something about a school's clients, a school's public, and a school's resources. What vision of the future do the people associated with the school have for the school and its children? Principals are naturally situated to explore the school's context and work with groups to develop commitment to a well-defined mission that contributes to realizing a shared vision.

Principals vary in how they relate to developing, communicating, and living a school mission. At one end of the continuum, some principals pay little or no attention to shared goals and do not frame tasks (their own or assignments for others) within a recognized shared purpose. No overall purpose or mission is evident in meetings with staff, parents, the public, or students. Neither is an overall purpose evident in school materials or actions of the principal. When asked, people associated with the school are unable to articulate a mission for the school, or they may attempt to share some ideas they have that others do not necessarily share. At worst, the school may be falling apart—literally and figuratively. Stress among staff members, student discipline problems, and difficulties in getting anything done may be evident. At best, the school may have the appearance of health because of limited disciplinary problems, a central role in the community, or the strong personality of the superintendent, principal, or informal leader(s). Relationships may be cordial or based on long-time acquaintance. Tradition and an attitude that things that aren't broken don't need fixing seem to prevail.

Exceptional principals work hard to find opportunities to form and discuss school goals, purposes, and mission with staff, parents, students, community members, and others in the district. Remember the pager study we told you about earlier? In one district that required principals to meet school buses in the morning, there was a notable range in the reflections of some principals on why they were doing it. Some saw it simply as an administrative function. Their presence was required to be sure the buses discharged an orderly group of students into the school. Others went beyond the immediate safety and discipline concerns. They used the time as an opportunity to orient students to the learning day. They inquired what students were doing in class, where they were in their studies, and clearly communicated the sense that they were interested in how students experience the school. These principals were doing mission.

The principal models the importance of the mission by making and supporting decisions that contribute to advancing the mission. For example, staff meetings include recognition of activities and decisions that further the mission. Collaborative staff work expends precious time and energies on projects supporting the mission. Conferences between teachers and the principal about classroom instruction are framed so that teachers become aware that their daily work with children communicates and advances the school's mission. Even apparently casual conversations with staff, students, parents, and others become opportunities for reminding everyone about "what is important around here." Students should become aware that the principal sees things from a particular point of view that clearly defines what matters at school.

Proposals presented to central office, outside funding groups, collaborating agencies, or the community should be framed within the school's mission. Certainly principals should turn every public speaking occasion, whether to a group of students or a local volunteer group, into an opportunity to increase awareness of their schools' missions. Recognition of excellent teaching by individuals or by teams may be turned into public opportunities to reinforce the centrality of instruction to a school's mission. Principals who see themselves as ambassadors of their schools' missions communicate excitement about the present and future possibilities for their schools. The mission is present on paper as well. Every document associated with the school, from letterhead to report cards to newsletters to yearbooks to curriculum guides, notes the school's mission. Letters home to parents containing either good or bad news frame that news within the mission. Principals who live their schools' missions communicate those missions orally, in writing, and through the bounce in their step as they go about their daily routines.

REFLECTING ON HOW TO DEVELOP, COMMUNICATE, AND LIVE A SCHOOL MISSION

Let's stop again for a moment to reflect on ways in which you can develop a more clearly focused school mission. Start by recalling one or more of your "AHA!" moments. How did each affect your educational philosophy?

Next, if you have gotten this far without doing so, write down your educational philosophy. Can you express it in 25 words without using jargon? Will everyone you meet understand it, including the coffee shop crowd, bus drivers, teachers, the superintendent, parents, and students?

Now, reflect on each of the questions below. You may find it useful to write down the answers as you read through the questions. Remember, you're not being graded on the answers you give, because there are no right answers—only answers that are right for you. Take time to reflect and respond thoughtfully to each one.

- What is your vision of the future for your school and the children it serves?

- What do you believe your school's mission to be?

- What answers do you get from teachers when you ask them to tell you the mission of your school? How varied are those responses? How alike or different are their responses from your conception of the mission?

- What responses do you get from students when you ask them about the mission of your school?

- What do parents think?

- What do others in your district, but outside your school, believe your school's mission to be?

- What evidence of a shared mission do you find around your school (in actions, language, symbols)?

- In what ways do your school's documents communicate the mission? Is the mission printed on documents? Does the tone of each document communicate the spirit of your printed mission or does the tone seem contrary to the printed mission statement?

- What evidence of your school's mission do you observe in formal faculty meetings and informal faculty conversations?

- How are students, good and less good, treated? Are they responded to, both positively and negatively, in ways reflective of your mission?

- In what ways do your disciplinary practices reinforce or subvert your school's mission?

- In the same vein, how are parents treated? Do drop-in parents and parents who attend conferences and special events leave with a sense that the mission was alive in their interaction with the school?

♦ To what extent does your curriculum, as intended and as implemented, support or ignore your school's mission? Does student assessment support or seem in contrast to the mission?

♦ What do you say and do on a regular basis that communicates a mission for your school?

♦ What specific opportunities could you use, which you do not use at this time, to communicate mission?

♦ How can you help your staff, parents, students, community members, and other administrators learn more about your school?

♦ How can you help your staff, parents, students, community members, and other administrators internalize and communicate your school's mission?

As we said earlier, there are no right answers to these questions. Similarly, there is no one right mission for all schools. The right mission depends on characteristics of the student body, teachers, others, and you!

Before we go to the next chapter, let's turn again to Nick Freeman and how he confronted the challenge of defining and communicating a coherent mission to his school.

NICK FREEMAN: RESTORING THE LOST MISSION OF WHITNEY ELEMENTARY SCHOOL

Nick became a teacher, in part, because as a child he had discovered other worlds through reading. At night he left the bedroom he shared with two brothers, traveling on long journeys courtesy of books. For Nick, education was also a means of finding independence and developing self-sufficiency, while still helping other people. All of this gave him a great deal of satisfaction. For Nick, education was an intensely personal experience.

Just how personal education was for him became clear when he thought about his "AHA" moment in education. Nick had been startled outside a downtown electronics store when an intense and very together young woman called out to him from just inside the door. The young woman started with, "You probably don't remember me, but." As Nick listened to the young woman thank him for giving her a chance, Nick swore to himself that he had never seen this person before. The substance of the conversation was that the young woman credited Nick with encouraging and supporting her at a time in her elementary school career when she was about to give up. She said that Nick had been the only teacher who cared. Others had labeled her a gangster by the time she was in fifth grade. Thanks to Nick's encouraging words, the young woman worked part-time during high school and had high enough SAT scores to attend a city college with partial financial support.

Though this young woman's story summed up the very reason Nick had wanted to be an educator, he was stunned and humbled by her story. Nick walked the ten blocks home in a daze. When he returned to his apartment, he located the box in his closet containing memorabilia from each of the classes he had taught. In a photo of his first class, he found a younger version of the woman he had just met. Obviously this person had changed a great deal. The "hood" in the picture was someone Nick had thought would land in jail, or, at best, in the unemployment line with a child on her hip before she was 18. Even though Nick the teacher had not intended to help this young woman, something he said without thinking about it or something he did without regard for consequences had somehow hit home. Shaken, Nick decided to never be flippant when talking to students. Obviously, you just never knew how a word or an action would affect a young and impressionable life.

Writing down his educational philosophy was a difficult task, especially in a limited number of words that everyone could understand. Nick wanted to be sure the philosophy was clear and one by which he could live. He finally wrote down his educational philosophy: "No child is a throwaway. Schools must contribute to children leading fulfilling and happy lives. The relationship between teachers and students is the most important in the school."

Nick had tried to share this philosophy during the numerous rounds of interviews that led to his being hired at Whitney. He assumed he was hired, in part, because most people working in the school shared that philosophy. Even so, he began to doubt that was so as he spoke during his first two months as principal with various teachers in the school. One teacher stood out as living the philosophy he was expressing, working overtime to save children whose lives seemed doomed from their early years. She was clearly one of the best first grade teachers in the city and had recently been honored for her success in teaching children to read. By contrast, it seemed to Nick that the fifth grade teachers considered "weeding out" and "sorting" children into potential successes and wastes of time to be their primary function. Between second and fourth grades, the dedication to children and their families seemed to gradually diminish from the attention given when children were in kindergarten and first grade. Nick discovered that the number of referrals to special education increased with each grade, so that more than 30% of all students had been referred for testing by the end of fourth grade.

After completing the "Guide to Reflection About Developing, Communicating, and Living a School Mission," Nick began informally asking teachers about Whitney's mission. It soon became clear that the staff of Whitney shared some ideas about the school as an important part of the community, but little else. Staff varied widely in their explanation of Whitney's relationship with students, the school's priorities, and the school's values. Eventually Nick found a few staff members who recalled a committee assigned to work on a mission statement a few years ago, when all schools in the city system had to do so. They were sure the librarian could help him locate the report prepared for a visit by the subdistrict superintendent and a team of central office directors. Probably that report would include the mission statement.

Most surprising to Nick was that no one seemed particularly disturbed that they could not verbalize a mission for Whitney. Although many teachers were aware that the central office was developing a set of standards for curriculum in all schools, they seemed unconcerned that Whitney was making no effort to become informed about those standards. The attitude seemed to be that the central office and state were meddling again, but would become discouraged or distracted and that this would be one of many passing reform initiatives. Nick found that although Whitney had been through cycles of adopting and abandoning trendy instructional innovations, these changes had been idiosyncratic outgrowths of individual staff member's interests. Some, such as whole language instruction, had stuck in first grade, but were dropped in later grades. Over the years, Whitney had drifted along a gentle wave of innovations and traditional ties to the community. Until recent changes in bussing and housing patterns had brought new minority groups to the school, parents and students seemed generally satisfied with Whitney Elementary School, although a few discontents regularly visited the office over a variety of situations concerning their children. Many of these currently petty but growing problems resulted from increasing diversity in the school community, something some parents were less than happy to see.

Nick knew that a mission that rested on a shelf somewhere in the library or the main office was no mission at all. He also knew that Whitney could not continue to drift, indifferent to changes in community, state, national, and international conditions and expectations. He had to help Whitney find its rudder. Nick would have to locate a strategy for engaging the Whitney stakeholders in developing a mission everyone could share, carry around, and explain to everyone they met.

Listening to the various responses he got when he asked people to describe the mission of Whitney led Nick to conclude that most people associated with the school knew surprisingly little about it. Though those questioned possessed clear ideas about their particular interests at Whitney, they knew very little about Whitney as a total organization. As long as the principal kept their classrooms well supplied and protected, each seemed content. Nick decided that for Whitney to be guided by a shared mission, totally new types of relationships had to emerge.

First, staff and others associated with the daily operations of Whitney had to develop new relationships with Whitney as an organization. That is, they had to learn about Whitney as a total organization of interdependent subsystems. They needed to understand how each part of the organization operated and contributed to Whitney's success as a school. They needed to understand how decisions in each subsystem could affect others. They needed to be knowledgeable about the facts rather than about assumptions they accepted as facts. Most staff members were completely unfamiliar with aspects of the budget, student demographics, student achievement, teacher workload, or staff motivation beyond the obvious.

Second, staff members needed to develop new relationships with each other. As long as they worked in isolation, interacting only with people with similar interests to protect, a collective mission and shared vision would never emerge. Nick felt staff members needed both to understand each other's perspectives and to step back from their interests long enough to see Whitney as a single organization with an overriding purpose for existing.

Thinking about these things on his own was of no value to Nick. He had to find a way to get people involved in the future of the school.

Nick began his exploration of how to get his school headed in a clear direction by getting to know the faculty and staff better. Even though he had worked as a teacher at Whitney for six years, Nick could not say that he really knew people well. His opinions, a mix of informal conversations and impressions gleaned at staff meetings and school-sponsored events, were grounded in little more than gut reactions. To start, he scheduled 30-minute interviews with every member of the faculty and staff in the early autumn. Everyone answered the same core set of questions. Tell me everything you can about your job at Whitney. Why did you come here and why do you stay? How do you feel when you come to work? What do you see as Whitney's purpose? What are Whitney's strengths and weaknesses? Inevitably these questions led to discussions that far exceeded 30 minutes. Nick discovered a lot about what made individuals tick and about alliances within the school.

Support staff expressed extreme devotion to Whitney and felt generally close to students. Many had seen two or three generations of families over the years in the school. The greatest challenge for support staff members was their relationship with teachers. They believed that teachers did not value them, that teachers saw them as second-class citizens. A few thought that teachers believed them to be spies for the administration.

Nick also arranged to meet with several groups of parents. Parents who were Whitney alumni loved the school but were anxious about changes in the makeup of classrooms that occurred over the past five or six years. Several made strong statements about not wanting their children mixing with "the others." Parents whose children had recently begun attending Whitney were impressed when they learned that Whitney graduates were more likely to complete high school than graduates of any other city elementary school. However, they were concerned that Whitney made few if any accommodations for their children's special needs, particularly in the area of language. A few pushed for Whitney to consider expanding bilingual programs similar to the magnet school recently started several miles away in another subdistrict.

Generally, Nick found a genuine love of Whitney by faculty, staff, and parents. When he talked with groups of students, he found a generally contented group of students, even though fifth graders were getting into fights more frequently. Mostly he saw the climate as pleasant, if not particularly exciting. The culture was symbolized by the school shield, artfully fashioned in tile inside the front door and representing the school's traditional place in the community. Whitney was part of the city's history. He decided he could use love of Whitney and the desire to be the best to leverage positive changes.

First, Whitney needed to understand itself. What were its strengths and weaknesses? Second, Whitney needed to know what it believed in and what its primary purpose for existing was. Third, Whitney needed a plan for approaching the future. That plan would emerge as Nick considered the options available to him for creating changes that would "take" at Whitney.

4

UNDERSTANDING AND PROMOTING SCHOOL CLIMATE AND CULTURE

The concepts of climate and culture originally developed within the literature of organizational psychology to deal with intangible aspects of the organization that had a significant influence on motivation and productivity. There is a great deal of conceptual overlap between the two of them, as the diagram below conveys. The terms "culture" and "climate" appear throughout the literature on schools and other organizations. Frequently they seem to be interchangeable.

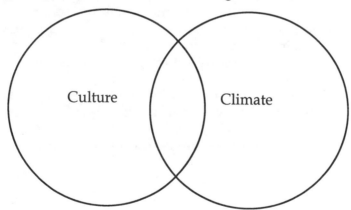

Nonetheless, as these research traditions evolved, "climate" has perhaps more often been associated with attitudinal, affective aspects and belief systems relative to the organization. "Culture" is perhaps more often used to describe behavioral expressions reflective of those attitudes and beliefs. In the same way that it is difficult to separate beliefs and actions, it is difficult to draw a clear distinction between climate and culture.

Successful building leadership requires understanding and manipulating both aspects of the school. As we said earlier, one of the first mistakes those new to leadership positions make is believing that their role is to tell people what to do. In reality, effective leaders create conditions under which people want to do what needs to be done. They create climates that motivate teachers, students, and parents. In that sense, the climate or culture of a school is the primary medium through which leadership operates within an organization. As a principal, you must leverage current climatic conditions and cultural expectations to get thing accomplished. You also need to know how to change damaging climates and discouraging cultures so that the climate supports collaboration and the culture encourages innovation.

BLOWING WINDS OF CLIMATE

One way to begin to understand the concept of school climate is simply to think about your school and ask yourself, "How is the weather around here?" Could you fairly categorize your school as a sunny, warm place where everyone likes to be and hates to leave? At the other end of the continuum, would you label your school "below freezing with strong chance of drifting snow, interfering with visibility"? How about "partly cloudy with a chance of severe storms"? Or maybe your school is "mild with occasional showers."

The day-to-day moods and attitudes of adults and students in the school offer cues to school climate. How do adults and students feel about coming to the school each day? What are the working relationships among adults and between the adults and the students? How do students treat each other? Are parents supportive or combative? Is the noise level the result of unrest or engagement? What do teachers and students do when they are not active in the classroom? In other words, what environment have we created for learning? How attractive, engaging, and effortless have we made learning through our use of facilities, interior and exterior decorations, accessibility of technology, attention to safety, continuity of learning time, and ease of interactions?

Climate both reflects and affects how people relate to each other and work with each other. A damaging climate, one subject to frequent hurricanes or tornadoes, causes school personnel to spend time stockpiling supplies and boarding up windows so that they will be safe when the next storm hits. Individuals worry about surviving the storms so much that they never get around to working with their neighbors to create something new. To survive, most find themselves competing with their neighbors for resources.

A supportive climate is bright and calm enough to encourage people to leave their shelters and engage in cooperative activities. A supportive climate experiences occasional showers and even storms, but everyone knows they are infrequent and harmless in the long run. Cleanup is a group effort. Climate essentially defines our working conditions, both physical and emotional. How well does the facility relate to and support learning? How well do working relationships promote positive interactions, sharing, risk taking, and celebrating individual and group accomplishments?

CUES TO UNDERSTANDING SCHOOL CLIMATE

- ◆ What is the mood of students and teachers when they enter the building?
- ◆ Do students and teachers look forward to coming to school?
- ◆ How do adults feel about going to work?
- ◆ How do students feel about going to school?
- ◆ How willing are teachers to put in extra time and effort?
- ◆ What kinds of discipline problems do we have?
- ◆ What do the adults complain about?
- ◆ What do the students complain about?
- ◆ How do we describe the relationships between the adults?
- ◆ How do we describe relationships between students?
- ◆ How formal are the interactions between students and teachers?
- ◆ How do parents feel about coming into the school?
- ◆ How visible are various types of adults before, after, and around school during the day?

- How many smiles and/or frowns do you count?
- What kind of talk goes on in the teacher's room or hallways?
- How frequently is instructional time interrupted?
- Is the school quiet, rowdy, or "busy" noisy?
- What do students do in the hallways?
- What shape is the physical plant in?

ARTIFACTS OF CULTURE

Culture encompasses the ways in which we express our values, beliefs, and attitudes. Think of culture as the outward signs of our civilization. Culture embodies the spoken and tacit rules about how we live, work, and play together. Culture is made up of the combination of ideas, customs, skills, and activities that occur and become repeated and refined over a period of years. School culture becomes obvious in our actions, in how we spend our time, and in what we reward. What motivates us to work, as individuals and as a school organization, both impacts and is impacted by the culture of our school. The school culture communicates to everyone associated with the school important messages about the value of their work, their rights, their responsibilities, and their status.

To get a handle on your school's culture, start by looking at the walls in the halls, classrooms, and offices. What do you see? Do you see school history? Do you see academic and/or athletic trophies of teams or individuals? Do you see student work? Do you see a bulletin board with current announcements? Do you see bare classroom walls? Now take a look at school publications, including your stationery. What do they communicate? Is there a logo? Do publications proclaim a sense of purpose, or are names and titles more prominently displayed?

What stories are told about the school? Is the school's history only that? Or is the school's history connected with the school's present through pictures and stories?

What does the school reward? How do we treat veteran teachers? How do we treat risk takers and people who are different? What do we publicly celebrate?

School cultures vary, understandably so. Schools are open systems. They take cues from a wide variety of sources, particularly local economic and social conditions and expectations. Because values differ and culture expresses values, cultures differ. A culture that values individual effort will be very different from a culture that values collaborative effort. A culture that values order will be very different from a culture that values spontaneity.

School cultures, like human cultures throughout the world, are distinguishable in part by their artifacts. Mention London, and many people will think of double-decker buses. For many, Rome is a city of churches and fountains, Venice a city of canals. The Taj Mahal comes quickly to mind when we think of India.

Think for a minute about your school as if it were a foreign country with which you are totally unfamiliar. Look through the eyes of a tourist for "cultural artifacts" that make it distinctive and memorable. How does it express its special character? Are there defining characteristics, or is it like another featureless subdivision, where even the street names seem repetitive? If you could return from this foreign land with just one item to use to explain this school, what would it be? What are the artifacts that symbolize the school culture?

CUES TO UNDERSTANDING SCHOOL CULTURE

◆ Who are our heroes?

◆ What are our stories about?

◆ What are our shared symbols?

◆ What is our history (and who cares)?

◆ What is rewarded around here?

◆ How are teachers treated?

◆ What do we display on the walls and in the halls?

◆ What do our written and printed materials communicate?

◆ What do we celebrate and how do we conduct our celebrations?

◆ What expectations do we communicate to students through what we say, do, and reward?

◆ What types of extracurricular activities do we sponsor?

◆ What percentage of students participates in extracurricular activities?

◆ How well (and equitably) do we pay sponsors of extracurricular activities?

◆ How do the adults group themselves to do their work?

◆ What language do students use toward each other and toward adults?

◆ What motivates us?

MOTIVATION

The last question brings us to a discussion of motivation because in our book, motivation is what culture and climate are about. That is, we want to create comfortable, positive school climates that motivate students to learn. We want to be aware of the power of school culture because it is the vehicle by which we motivate teachers, students, and parents and engage them actively in the learning process. Motivation plays a key role in the culture and climate of schools (Maehr & Braskamp, 1986). The relationship among an individual's primary motivation and organizational culture and climate determines to a great extent how members of the school organization feel about and behave within the school.

The concept of motivation applies equally well to organizations as to individuals. Just as you know people who appear primarily motivated by acquiring power through money, so you know schools that must win every competition, sports or otherwise, in which they engage. In the school's case, the search for power simply takes another form.

Consequently, the link between motivation and climate is an intimate one. It is also a useful one to explore further. But how should we think about motivation?

Maehr and Braskamp (1986) provide a useful way to think about motivation as having practical implications for describing and working with the climate of organizations. Although there are theoretically many different ways to classify or describe what motivates people, Maehr and Braskamp use four primary dimensions to describe motivation and climate or cultural features of organizations: accomplishment, recognition, power, and affiliation. A brief description of each is useful in further understanding the intimate connection between motivation and culture.

ACCOMPLISHMENT

Individuals who are motivated by accomplishment are very involved in their work. They want the job to be challenging, exciting, and fun. They feel most comfortable and proud of themselves when they do things other people cannot do or when they solve problems that seem to stump other people. They may feel dissatisfied when their freedom to explore new solutions to problems is restricted. It is important to them that their jobs provide variety and stimulation. When work becomes routine, they can quickly become bored and uninterested. They generally identify themselves as "self-starters," people who like challenges and spend time thinking of new ways to improve themselves. They take pride in what they do and work hard to improve job skills. They may often find themselves working extra hours and putting in time when others do not, just to meet their own personal performance standards.

School climates that emphasize accomplishment value excellence and quality in what they do. They support new ideas and innovative problem solving. Administrators and teachers have a high degree of freedom and autonomy to be creative. People do not worry about being punished if their ideas fail. Quality education is emphasized with a clear focus on excellence, both of process and outcome. The perception of employees, students, and other stakeholders is that this school is the best.

RECOGNITION

Individuals for whom recognition is important work hardest when they receive respect and external acknowledgment for their work. They are likely to do their best when they have the encouragement and support of others. Financial reward is also valued strongly because it represents a very significant (if not the most significant) indicator of success and status. Individuals motivated by recognition seek high paying and high status jobs. They will work hard for these visible symbols of success. They interpret these symbols as representing their worth to others.

A school climate that values recognition sees individuals and groups of teachers and students as being winners. Such a school encourages and rewards high productivity. The need to work hard to accomplish goals is reinforced. Expectations and rewards are clear and consistent. Frequent and elaborate public ceremonies glorify both the individuals who succeed and their school. Press releases and photos featuring students and teachers who have succeeded in large and small ways are common. Memos from the principal to students for landing parts in the annual musical and to teachers for being elected to a state level office in a professional association are the norm.

POWER

Power has to do with competition. Individuals motivated by power are ambitious, competitive people who work hard to get ahead. They like to be in charge and strive for leadership and positions in which they can be in control of other people. They prefer and seek competitive situations in which there are clear winners and losers. Popularity is less important to them than achievement. They often feel that the best way to help others is to get them to do it their way (the right way). Such individuals either channel their competitive needs into productive goals, like raising the most funds for a good cause, or alienate themselves from coworkers and friends.

School cultures that value power emphasize competition. Contests determine winners. Contests for all desirable rewards, including promotions, raises, resources, and public recognition characterize a competitive culture. Grade levels and classrooms compete to see who is the best. This is true regardless of whether "best" means collecting cans of food for the poor, reading books to win a pizza party, or scoring highest on the state achievement test. Conflict may be a byproduct of a power-based culture, but in this culture, conflict is seen as inevitable and even healthy. Competition seems a desirable means of encouraging ambitious adults and children to excel.

AFFILIATION

Individuals who are motivated by affiliation genuinely like other people. They care deeply about interpersonal relationships. These people enjoy opportunities to work closely with others. They seek warm, supportive, nurturing environments. They are energized by the presence of others. They share information easily and involve others in decisions. Good working and social relationships are so important that individuals motivated by affiliation will sacrifice personal gain to save a friendship.

Schools that value affiliation have supportive cultures characterized by trust and respect. Sharing information, collaborative decision making, and cooperative problem solving are normal operating procedures. Teachers and students feel that the school really cares about them as unique individuals. Words such as caring, sharing, trusting, and cooperative describe the working environment.

What motivates you and how is that motivation reflected in the type of climate you create in your school? Let's use this framework to assess the relative importance you place on each of these four orientations. As you work through the checklist, be reflective and honest with yourself.

MOTIVATION SELF-ASSESSMENT

How important is accomplishment to me? Do I

- ◆ actively seek ways in which the school can be more effective, including seeking suggestions from teachers, staff, and students?
- ◆ strive for excellence in everything I do?
- ◆ try new things on a regular basis?
- ◆ push others to do a really good job?
- ◆ encourage others to try new things, even if some past efforts have failed?

How important is recognition to me? Do I

- ◆ put complimentary notes in faculty and staff members' mailboxes regarding little and big things I notice them doing?
- ◆ try to make everyone associated with the school feel important?

- evaluate staff on their work performance, trying to balance the positive with the negative?
- hold teacher and student award assemblies?
- provide regular feedback to faculty and staff about how they are doing?

How important is power to me? Do I

- encourage competition among teachers, grade levels, and departments?
- view a certain amount of tension and conflict as healthy?
- actively seek to work with individuals who hold powerful positions inside and outside the school?
- seek opportunities for students and teachers to compete with neighboring schools?
- compare my school's test scores and athletic winnings to those of other area schools?

How important is affiliation to me? Do I

- tend to needs of faculty and students that sometimes go beyond what most principals are expected to do?
- treat faculty and staff like adults who can make good decisions for themselves?
- trust faculty and staff?
- make sure faculty and staff know as much about what is going on as I do?
- engage in frequent, informal conversations with faculty, staff, and students?

This short self-assessment activity helps further clarify the close connection between climate and motivation, how motivation affects climate, and how climate influences motivation. Although climate problems occur when faculty members' personal motivations clash, a faculty that has been together for several years is likely to have settled on an unspoken acknowledgment of "how things are done around here."

Consider a school in which the prevailing culture is one of affiliation, one that puts interpersonal relationships before all else. An administrator who is motivated by competition introduces high stakes contests in an effort to improve student achievement. Failure to understand and respect the culture of the school may result not only in unimproved (if not decreased) student achievement, but also in transforming school climate from productive to dysfunctional.

School climate is a product, in large part, of the coherence between a leader's motivation, philosophy, and vision, and that of the majority of others associated with the school. The greater the coherence, the more positive the school climate. The greater the diversity, the more turbulent the school climate.

LEADING AND MOTIVATING CHANGE

Principals probably make more impact on teacher motivation and student achievement through their impact on school climate and culture than through attention to any other aspect of schools. In this respect, principals affect students by affecting the working conditions of other adults in the school. Roland Barth (1990) reminds us that, "What needs to be improved about schools is their culture, the quality of interpersonal relationships, and the nature and quality of learning experiences" (p. 45). Studies by Maehr and Braskamp (1986) demonstrated that leaders can affect motivations of people working in organizations by manipulating culture and climate. Echoing this message, Maehr and Parker, in a 1993 article for *Phi Delta Kappan*, write about the leader's role in shaping culture:

> References to leadership and culture roll easily off educators' lips these days, but not everyone understands these terms in the same way. From our perspective, two points regarding leadership and culture are critical. First, leaders are simply not the captives of culture. They can and do affect the lives and learning of students, which is their ultimate responsibility. Thus, the nature and impact of school culture must be of major concern to school leaders.

Conscientious attention to scheduling, accounting, or routinizing, while necessary, is not sufficient if a school is to become a place where student learning and personal growth are the objectives. Attention must be given to the beliefs about students, teaching, and learning and how these are embodied in the events and routines of the school. This is where a principal who wants to make change should focus energy. (p. 233)

Principals new to a building are frequently expected to bring about change. Sometimes that change is well defined. More often a need for change is clear, but no vision of the desired alternative has been developed or presented. These days a principal may simply be told that the staff needs to work together better. What you believe about change will affect how you go about making changes.

Training leaders to make change is a topic that fills library shelves with theoretical solutions for doing so. However, most change theories involve one of two simple approaches: change people's behaviors or change people's values. At the bottom line, institutionalizing change requires doing both. The question is where to start.

CHANGING ATTITUDES AND VALUES

Some believe that the most humane and effective way to change a school is to deal first with the concerns, interests, and values of people working in the school, which is a long process. Modeling is a concrete way to start. The principal's visible actions, as public expressions of the principal's values, have an undeniable impact on the attitudes of those around the principal. A principal who believes in life-long learning and who discusses current readings with faculty, formally or informally, may eventually cause others to publicly value their own learning. A principal who believes in experiential learning and works with a teacher and the community to arrange special experiences for a group of students may inspire others to adopt such strategies. A principal who values relationships and so treats others with obvious courtesy may inspire others to behave cordially.

Although a leader's modeling is an important influence on transforming climate, by itself it is seldom enough to induce genuine change. Fundamental change in our values and norms and heroes involves serious study of why we do what we do, what we would like to be doing, and how to get there.

In a nutshell, changing school climate involves vision. It also involves two assumptions about people as individuals and their attitudes about their work found in the field of organization development. First, individuals desire personal growth and development and prefer a supportive and challenging work environment. Second, most people desire and are capable of making a higher level of contribution to the organization than most work environments permit (French & Bell, 1990).

Changing attitudes means discussing personal and educational philosophies, visions of education, and perceptions of school mission as a starting point for developing a shared vision and common mission for the school. Although all the talk is exhausting and development of vision and mission might seem like ends in themselves, nothing really matters unless people associated with the school choose to begin to behave differently. Behaviors must be in line with what we say a school should be (vision) and what we say we want to accomplish (mission). Once a principal has worked with internal and external stakeholders to change the school on paper, that is only the first step. The principal must subsequently redouble efforts to assure that the vision and mission walk and talk all around the school and throughout the community. What goes on in classrooms, administrative decisions, interpersonal relationships, and resource allocations provide the real test of a fundamental change in the school's climate.

Consider a principal who believes strongly in the importance of collaboration in decision-making, instruction, and learning. This principal may have a vision of a school in which a leadership team makes long-range plans, interdisciplinary teaching is the norm, and cooperative learning is the primary learning strategy. Realizing that attempting to force teachers to share in decision-making and alter their approach to teaching would be unsuccessful, the principal decides to approach the changes by working through core values held by teachers. Changing values means intensive staff development, nurturing of trusting and open relationships, rewarding risk-taking, and realizing that visible results may not emerge for several years. In this case, the principal uses a consultant to open dialogue, engages the faculty in reading groups, finds time for team planning, supports a trial period in which a small group experiments with the ideas, facilitates planning for inclusive school governance, and finds ways to showcase successful innovations. To do so takes years, constant reference to the vision, and making decisions consistent with that vision. If administrators and the public have patience, changing the values (and so the culture) will, in the long run, result in lasting changes in behaviors, particularly those associated with teaching and learning. Eventually, the holdouts who approach change from the "I'll believe it when I see it" position adopt their changed behaviors as everyday behaviors or leave the school for one more congenial. Rooms will open up. Relationships between teachers and with students will become less formal. The school's approach to discipline will change. The use of time will become flexible. These changes in climate make the changes in culture, which have been evolving over several years, visible and tangible.

CHANGING BEHAVIOR

The other approach focuses on changing behaviors first. Results may appear to be more immediate. Changing the cleanliness of a building, for example, may result in students and teachers being more careful at first. For this to last for even one semester, the change agent can never let down the cleanliness guard. Hallways and classrooms must always be cleaned to a high standard. Vandals must always be punished. Students and organizations that contribute to the neat appearance of the building must be consistently and constantly rewarded. In the long run, students and faculty may come to value a well-maintained physical plant. Only then will additional improvements, initiated by others than the principal, become likely. When changes in behaviors result in changes in values, only then does the change become part of the normal operations and expectations of the school.

Another example of beginning to make changes by starting with behavior occurs when a principal alters the relationship between school and home. This most likely begins with things the principal controls, like instituting a quarterly newsletter, training parent volunteers, and evaluating teachers on the frequency of their positive contacts with students' families. If continued and reinforced over time, these changes in behaviors could lead to changes in teachers' and parents' attitudes about parental involvement with the school. This change could eventually lead to a subsequent change in values that causes others to initiate new collaborations.

Principals send messages every day about their acceptance or rejection of the current school climate and culture. Principals impact climate every day as they visibly manage conflict, interact with teachers, spend time in the hallways and office, communicate with office staff, deal with the public, meet with parents, and mentor new teachers. No one person affects the climate of the school more than the principal. If you doubt this, find a school with a new principal and you'll likely find a school with an altered climate.

The very act of changing leaders changes the mood of the school. Other visible changes stir the climate barometer, especially if a new leader makes them. One new principal immediately improved the climate of a school. She made it more comfortable than it had been in years by moving the principal's office out of an inaccessible corner behind a fortress of counters and secretaries. Students, parents, and teachers now had direct access from a well-traveled hallway. She made the office inviting, covering the nondescript carpet with a large pastel rug. Although she made many other improvements, the rug became the symbol of her emphasis on relationships. Staff commented on how inviting the office looked, and groups of students (and some groups of teachers) sat on the rug during visits with the principal. Rolling up the rug at the end of her tenure at the school symbolized another change in the culture, leaving a vacuum to be filled in yet a different way by the new leader. Even seemingly simple actions by the principal, such as new decor or location of the principal's office, rearranging the staff lounge, or redirecting traffic in front of the school affect school climate. Consistently rewarding valued behaviors, such as interdepartmental planning, may cause those in the school who hold similar values, but who never felt safe to express or act on them before, to assume informal leadership roles. Never assume that what you say or do, no matter how insignificant it seems, has no impact on the very mood or climate of the school organization.

Principals find this kind of change, which is fundamental to the success of the school, very challenging. Even so, unless a principal finds a means of affecting climate and culture, the more things change the more they stay the same. Teachers, staff, students, and parents may delight at superficial changes. However, the more important work of schools, the interaction between students and teachers in classrooms, will change only when the core values of those doing the teaching and learning change.

Remember, a positive climate should be leveraged, not challenged, for change. Do your homework about a building before taking action lest you upset the climate apple cart and are forced to leave before you can have a fundamental influence.

AWARENESS CHECK ON CLIMATE AND CULTURE

- ◆ Think of yourself as a meteorologist and your school as a region of the country. How would you describe the weather for tomorrow? Is this prediction characteristic of nearly every day? Or does the weather change daily? In what ways do you contribute to the stability or instability of the climate?

- ◆ List the various stakeholder groups associated with your school. Next to each group, list their key values. How do these values affect your school?

- ◆ List one to five words expressing the central values of your school as a whole. What label could you give to easily describe this culture?

- ◆ What conditions and artifacts might you expect to be evident in a school with a culture that values academic achievement and has a climate of cool relationships among faculty and between faculty and students?

- ◆ What conditions and artifacts might you expect to be evident in a school with a culture that values inclusion of all children in all activities and a warm friendly climate?

- What motivates you on the job? How is your primary motivation evident in the things you say and do?

- What motivates most of your faculty? How is their primary motivation(s) evident inside and outside classrooms?

- In what ways does your primary motivation conflict with or support the norms of your school?

- How might you use what you know about aspects of culture, climate, and motivation to see that your next job is in a school that "fits" you?

- How might you use what you know about aspects of culture, climate, and motivation to perform the role of change-agent in a school?

ELIZABETH HARRIS: TAKING THE PULSE OF CENTRAL HIGH

Elizabeth's first year at Central was hectic. She arrived less than four weeks before school started. That time was filled with last minute hiring, calendar revisions, extracurricular concerns, building readiness efforts, copy machine contracts, a back-to-school letter, budget revisions, district meetings, new student and teacher orientations, and planning for the first faculty meeting and in-service days. Names and faces collided with deadlines and requirements in her dreams as her subconscious attempted to sort the confusion she experienced consciously each day. Throughout her first year as principal, Elizabeth made heroic efforts to get in classrooms, lead straightforward faculty meetings, and support faculty needs. Her open-door policy had been successful if measured by her need to communicate her accessibility and interest in everyone at Central. It had been a disaster if measured by her need to complete all her work, including getting back to parents and others who telephoned or wrote letters rather than show up in person.

Elizabeth decided she could have an open door and still manage her time better. Each day she designated a different hour when, short of an emergency of extraordinary proportions, she would open mail and return phone calls without interruption. She also blocked out Fridays, refusing to make appointments of any kind unless they were command performances at Central Office or essential to the well-being of students. Fridays she would visit classrooms and be available to students during their lunch periods.

Elizabeth also decided that if she was going to lead Central into the future, she had to take charge of making the school more collaborative. Her first year convinced Elizabeth that collaboration doesn't occur naturally. She was the one who had to make it happen.

During the summer before her second year at Central, Elizabeth met with each faculty and support staff member willing to give up some time to speak with her. When school started, she met with small groups of students.

For the most part, each staff member viewed his or her niche as the apex of the school's mission. The athletic director referred to the importance of creating a competitive spirit, while the chair of the foreign language department discussed the importance of developing understanding of cultural diversity and international community. The director of counseling services cited the mission as getting more than 85% of each graduating class into college. One parent said she believed the mission of Central was to be a better school than the other public schools in the community. An honor student took a stab at describing Central in terms of involving everyone in everything to prepare everyone for life. A successful but less high achieving student merely shrugged. On the whole, though, Elizabeth discovered that students were much more certain about the purpose of Central than were faculty. Most assumed that Central prepared kids for college. Those without college aspirations felt free to goof off because they didn't see themselves as fitting in with their image of Central.

At the opening faculty meeting of her second year at Central, Elizabeth asked all faculty and staff members to complete a school climate inventory with which she had become familiar in graduate school. The primary purpose of the inventory was to assess faculty and staff perceptions of the ways in which they and the principal worked together.

When the data, collected and reported anonymously, returned from processing by the publisher of the climate instrument, Elizabeth discovered some things about her leadership and about those she was hired to lead. First, she found that her informal assessment regarding the school's sense of mission was right on the mark. Though she had tried to talk to people about her ideas for Central, few had embraced those ideas or accepted them as relevant to their own view of Central. Scores were low on items associated with talking about mission and goals, administrator visibility, and recognition of good teaching.

Scores in the other areas were low as well. Faculty and staff did not see any relationship between school purposes and curriculum or any coordination of curriculum with assessment. The only places others saw leadership affecting their work were in areas associated with demanding more effort or checking to see that staff worked to capacity. Overall, the climate survey reflected little participation in the school beyond the classroom. Teachers and support staff obviously did not feel valued by the administration, and they seldom discussed teaching issues with each other. Most answered in ways that suggested the climate of Central was very competitive. This competitive climate affected the work of faculty and staff. They felt the administration traditionally had valued conflict and competition and took the attitude that winners would be rewarded. Clearly they were not yet convinced that Elizabeth's values were any different.

Despite these negative trends, those completing the survey felt generally satisfied with their work at Central. The highest-scoring items had to do with working with others in the school. Most felt loyal to Central, and they indicated that it would take a great deal for them to leave Central for work in other schools.

Elizabeth shared the data from the climate survey with the faculty and staff at the second staff meeting of the school year. Elizabeth found herself grateful that a practice at Central for the past four years had been to start school late one day each month. That way staff meetings could be held while everyone was fresh and without interference from extracurricular duties. No one doubted the importance of mission, but everyone was amazed at the many different ways in which Central's mission was characterized during the discussion. A light bulb seemed to go on that morning, as past differences that had seemed insoluble were illuminated by the obvious confusion about Central's mission. The feedback regarding motivation and relations between administrators, staff, and faculty led to lively discussion all day long. People who had not talked with each other for some time now had something to discuss. It was clear that people at Central valued each other's goodwill, and points of view all became increasingly clear.

Elizabeth proposed to the faculty and staff that Central commit to a year-long process of self-examination and reflection. A facilitator from a nearby university volunteered to work with Central, not as an expert who would provide Central with answers to its questions, but as a neutral group processor. The staff meeting closed with the decision to elect a core planning team consisting of six faculty members, two staff members, two parents, and two students. The principal would also be an ex officio member of the core team.

The first meeting of the core team began at 7:00 A.M. Substitute teachers and temporary office help allowed the core team to meet until 11:00 A.M. The facilitator engaged the group in an hour of exercises that some thought frivolous at first. The activities helped core team members get to know each other and each other's values in ways quite different from those resulting from daily contact or lack of contact. At the end of the first hour, teachers gained respect for the values held by nonteachers. Parents learned how important student well being was to both faculty and staff members. School personnel discovered that parents held the school in high regard, but they were suspicious of any efforts to change a system in which their children were doing well. All found that students, too, were suspicious of change that affected them directly, even as they advocated it for teachers and administrators.

Discovering Central's mission became the first big task for the core team. The mission would not become clear through the use of any crystal ball or inspiration. The core team decided to get some issues out into the open. Even Elizabeth had trouble accurately describing how things currently were. Two types of data needed to be explored: data about how the school works and data about how people work within the school.

A few things about how the school works could be easily studied. Elizabeth opened "the books." She shared all available information about the budget, salary categories, curriculum, extracurricular participation, student demographics, student achievement, and teacher-to-student load. Data about some other things still needed to be gathered. What were the belief's around which a mission could be built? Did inequities in faculty workload and rewards for work beyond the classroom exist? What caused faculty, who value the goodwill of others, to work competitively rather than collaboratively?

The core team and its facilitator began to move in several directions simultaneously. They arranged to use the first major in-service day of the semester to engage the entire faculty and staff as well as parent and student representatives in generating a list of beliefs on which to base Central's mission. They also worked with a graduate student from the university who was specializing in organizational development to study the causes of the competitive work climate. Another graduate student worked with the committee to design a study of faculty classroom and nonclassroom workload and reward structures. The core team urged everyone in the school to cooperate with the studies. Individual sources of data would remain anonymous. All responses to interviews and surveys would be confidential. Everyone understood that the data belonged to the school and would not be reported elsewhere in any way that would identify Central. The core team clearly intended that the data be used to make decisions, not judgments.

Elizabeth was heartened by the core team's quick ownership of the year's data gathering and decision-making process. She used her interpersonal skills to work with the university faculty member as a cofacilitator of the staff development day. Small groups worked throughout the day to generate, categorize, condense, and prioritize beliefs. Finally, a list of ten beliefs was ready for examination by the greater Central High School community.

By Thanksgiving the core team had reviewed comments about the beliefs, made revisions, and began trying to summarize the beliefs in the form of a shared mission statement. The core team was determined to use a minimum number of words in the mission. The mission had to be one everyone could easily recite in his or her head and in their hearts. Elizabeth was very excited when the core team unveiled their carefully crafted statement and asked for feedback from students, parents, and others. By Valentine's Day Elizabeth and representatives of the core team presented Central's mission and beliefs to the school board.

Proposed Mission of Central High School

The mission of Central High School is to educate young people for the worlds of work, higher education, and democratic citizenship.

Proposed Beliefs of Central High School

At Central, we believe in diversity, equity, individualism, and collaboration. Central High School should:

Serve the diverse needs of learners inside and outside the classroom;

Encourage individual development and freedom of expression in a secure environment;

Establish a climate of respect and trust;

Engage in a collaborative process to secure resources necessary to accomplish its mission;

Create staffing plans that recognize individual strengths and contributions to the mission;

Graduate students who have significant opportunities for employment or continuing education.

Throughout the fall Central experienced a surge of creative energy. The focus on beliefs and mission seemed to build on everyone's sense of loyalty. The energy was also fueled by a sense of urgency. Central could not be allowed to be portrayed in the minds of faculty and staff or in the eyes of others as anything but the best. Drifting with no sense of mission certainly made Central's image vulnerable.

Elizabeth knew that the careful selection of words forming the beliefs and mission would be a cynically remembered exercise if some of the ways in which the school and its people worked didn't change. She hoped that the graduate students would present useful data to the core team. If their data collection efforts failed or were misunderstood, she would have to find other ways to get to the heart of important dissatisfactions lurking beneath Central's surface.

In early October, the core team dealt with faculty and staff perceptions of the working processes of Central High School. Because issues of competitiveness and rewards were emotionally charged issues, every adult in the school had been individually interviewed. Questions, agreed upon by the core team, were based on Weisbord's Six-Box Model, which provides a framework for diagnosing an organization's formal and informal systems (Weisbord, 1976). Each had answered questions about the school's leadership, purpose, helpful mechanisms, structures, rewards, and relationships.

One graduate student reported that, until the work began in the fall, faculty and staff had no shared purpose. Nevertheless, they were hopeful that the interview process could identify a shared purpose. Several feared that turf battles would get in the way. An overwhelming number saw the lack of shared purpose as the primary cause behind the divisions between faculty and staff. A majority complained that the merit pay system encouraged competition rather than collaboration and had not resulted in the anticipated surge of excellence. Tangible rewards, such as salary for regular and extra duties, seemed inadequate and inequitable.

Two weeks later, the second graduate student reported on faculty workload, which was another emotionally charged issue. Faculty work had been defined by the core team as possibly encompassing a combination of (1) classroom instruction, (2) nonclassroom activities related to academic courses, library and media, (3) student services such as counseling and student advisement, and (4) committee work both related to and unrelated to instruction. Classroom instruction and some aspects of indirect instruction had been calculated based on records of teaching and nonteaching assignments. Other data came from faculty interviews, administrative reporting, and records of committee assignments and extracurricular contracts. The analysis considered individual, faculty as a whole, work categories, paid and unpaid assignments, and gender.

When the analyses were complete, data confirmed that faculty had every right to generally feel overworked. Nearly 85% of faculty worked more than 40 hours each week because of a combination of regular and extraduty assignment. More than half worked more than 60 hours every week. Only slightly more than 50% of faculty time was spent on classroom instruction. The rest of faculty time was spent primarily on nonclassroom support of students' academic endeavors and student advisement. A great deal of time was split between extracurricular duties and various committees not focused on the classroom. Not surprisingly, the majority of extra pay went for athletics, not for additional academic or organizational responsibilities. Significantly more men than women received extra pay. Women held 75% of the unpaid assignments for committees and support of academics outside the classroom.

Elizabeth and core team members found themselves in a quandary. Now that they had real data concerning the reasons people found it difficult to work together, what were they to do about it?

They began by mapping what they had learned against their beliefs. How did their actions support or undermine their beliefs? The current system of individual merit pay seemed to defeat any notion of collaboration. Were merit pay and equity complementary or competing ideas? Paying for excellent work in extracurricular activities while expecting excellent work on academic committees before and after school to occur without pay seemed inequitable. A few teachers expressed concern that issues of excellence were at risk as well, with an emphasis on excellence in sports leading to a potential slighting of academics. The fact that nearly everyone was already running as fast as possible also threatened any collaborative efforts that would require even more time.

The core team worked to put words to the climate and culture. Certainly it was one of excellence. Doing well, being the best was important. Achievement and recognition motivated the school. The halls were full of trophies, both academic and athletic. The climate was cordial but reserved, the way one star athlete is to another just before the competition. Teachers put in a lot of extra time. Few discipline problems disrupted classes. Talk tended to focus on competitions. Complaints, by both students and adults, were mostly about time.

The core team shared what they had learned and discussed at the November staff meeting, the same meeting at which beliefs and a draft mission were reviewed. The discussion centered on continuing to value excellence. However, issues of competition permeated all discussions. Opening the budget to scrutiny revealed unchallenged historical patterns of high and low budget for departments over the years at constant rates, although the number of faculty and students and classrooms had changed. The curriculum had become less a function of planned change than of competition by departments for students.

The larger the number of students taking a department's courses, the greater the number of sections and teachers acquired by that department. Student achievement had long been reported in terms of SAT and ACT scores. Scrutiny of the scores caused many to fear that Central was losing its edge, as scores had been declining the past five years. Most, though not all, believed that the climate would have to be more warm and supportive, more receptive to diverse opinions, and more rewarding of group efforts. Central's internal climate would have to become collaborative so that Central's students could be externally competitive. Excellence, as an expression of cultural value, would have to take on new meaning.

Elizabeth ended her second year at Central on an optimistic note. The faculty, staff, students, and parents now seemed to view Central through different lenses. Nearly nine months of working to establish a set of beliefs, shared mission, and expectations regarding culture and climate had brought together individuals and groups who had previously each supported Central in their own ways. Now a new energy surrounded Central. Could she capitalize on it to implement and institutionalize a new way of working at Central High School?

5

KNOWING, FOCUSING, DEVELOPING, AND DELIVERING CURRICULUM

Much has been made in the past ten years of the notion that principals should first and foremost be instructional leaders; that is, principals who want to improve their schools must find ways to improve the curriculum and the ways in which curriculum becomes implemented through classroom instruction. Michael Fullan, writing in *What's Worth Fighting for in the Principalship* (1988), encourages principals to "Focus on Something Important Like Curriculum and Instruction" (p. 27). According to Fullan, priorities result from juggling political and educational concerns. Principals must establish priorities if they are to avoid overload yet get something that matters accomplished. Every school, regardless of the leader's philosophy, regardless of the shared vision, and regardless of the carefully selected words expressing a school's mission, has at its heart one purpose: academic success of students. Consequently, curriculum must be on the principal's short list of priorities. Academic success is measured by different criteria in a wide variety of contexts. Even so, learning, promotion, and graduation of students is the primary business of schools.

Two major factors controlled by schools are central to student achievement: teachers and curriculum. Principals are in charge of how teachers teach. Principals are also in charge of what gets taught. No one doubts that curriculum is vital to student success. Unfortunately, managing curriculum is difficult. Curriculum resembles the old science fiction monster, the "Blob." Just when the heroes thought they knew how to control it (or at least escape it), the Blob would ooze through new cracks in the defenses.

So it is with curriculum. Only the constant attention that is difficult for a principal to furnish keeps it within bounds. Failure to attend to curriculum encourages mutations stimulated by outside forces such as textbook and software publishers, hardware vendors, professional associations, the latest workshop, the state department of education, funding sources, and special interest groups. Whether any of these influences should have any bearing is, at least in part, in the control of principals.

WHAT IS CURRICULUM?

Being in charge of a building's curriculum is made difficult by the multiple personalities assigned to curriculum. How is curriculum defined in your district? What aspect or aspects of the district definition are a principal's responsibility?

A rather narrow perspective on curriculum defines it as subject matter or content expected to be taught at each grade. This point of view emphasizes a sequence of knowledge and ideas in selected subject areas through the school years. Embodied within this concept is the notion of a leadership academic curriculum. Principals operating from this definition of curriculum may pay limited attention to instructional strategies because they often assume that professional teachers will select appropriate means of delivery. They view the principal's job as ensuring that teachers understand the organization of learning across grades and within subject areas. Their job, as they see it, is to protect the integrity of this organization of curriculum.

Others view curriculum as extending beyond what should be taught to encompass how it should be taught as well. This less restrictive definition encroaches on teacher's autonomy more than the prior definition by managing not only what is taught, but how teachers deliver content. From this perspective, curriculum is a series of guidelines or plans prescribing what is to be taught, how it is best taught, and what the student is supposed to know and be able to do. This sounds familiar to teachers and administrators exposed in their preservice and graduate studies to the work of Ralph Tyler, who wrote about behavioral objectives, learners' needs, and curriculum planning a half-century ago. Similarly, the controversial outcomes-based education movement champions this approach to curriculum, although it takes a very different view from the behaviorists of how teachers should teach.

An even more expansive definition sees curriculum as a series of expectations and potential experiences vertically and horizontally linking subject matter and grade levels. This approach sees curriculum not as discreet skills and knowledge to be acquired at specified grades. Instead, this definition ascribes overlap, spiraling, and interdisciplinary natures to knowledge. This approach to curriculum considers the arts and internship experiences as essential to graduating well-rounded students. Instead of considering curriculum as one of many discrete building blocks of a good school, those who adopt this approach to curriculum see the school as a network of many interdependent subsystems. Consequently, changes to any of the school's subsystems are deliberated in light of their potential affects on the curriculum. This more humanistic approach encourages a range of experiences and problem-solving challenges that integrate student interests with planned content. Personnel not normally considered responsible for the curriculum may be drawn into its delivery at various times. For example, school cooks may participate in a unit on family living, catering, or careers. The assistant principal might be found playing the role of Officer Krupke in a production of "West Side Story," demonstrating the value of the fine arts in people's lives regardless of their vocations.

A still more comprehensive definition characterizes curriculum as the sum of structured learning experiences of learners. This portrayal includes extracurricular activities as well as formal classroom instruction. This definition does not require linking areas of the academic curriculum with each other or with the extracurricular curriculum. But it does acknowledge that a lot of learning takes place after the formal school day ends. This "second shift," especially in comprehensive high schools, is for some students and their parents the primary purpose of school and requires at least as much careful attention and planning as the academic curriculum.

The definition of curriculum from which you operate naturally constrains your understanding of the purpose of instruction. What are teachers in your school really trying to accomplish? Are they coaching students to achievement of behavioral objectives in discrete subjects? Are they working to produce students who can demonstrate mastery of outcomes, through various means? Are teachers striving to inspire creative thinking? Or do teachers want students to recall culturally relevant and useful facts? Is the purpose of teaching to prepare students for the worlds of work and higher education? Or is the primary purpose of teaching to produce literate citizens?

Curriculum presents numerous critical decision opportunities for principals and their school communities. Thinking about curriculum and how to provide leadership with respect to curricular issues leads naturally to an important series of questions. First, do you clearly understand and share an operational definition of curriculum with the teachers in your school? Second, do you agree on a vision and mission for your school, and can you find ways to directly connect the curriculum to vision and mission? Third, what role do curriculum standards at the national, state, and local level play in the design, delivery, and evaluation of your curriculum? What approaches to instruction best deliver the curriculum? What technologies contribute to student mastery of the curriculum? How should student achievement of the curriculum be assessed?

BEGIN WITH THE VISION AND MISSION

Curriculum, how you see it, how you plan for it, and how you implement it presents opportunities to consolidate vision, mission, and philosophies in ways that positively affect children and distinguish your school. Curriculum design is a natural starting point for developing an expectation of teamwork and tapping of teacher expertise. Curriculum design work also creates a natural forum for putting vision and mission before faculty and parents.

Regardless of how curriculum is defined in a given district, principals must insist that the content and strategies associated with curriculum directly relate to each school's vision and mission. If a school does not have a shared and publicly professed vision and mission, time spent working on curriculum will be wasted. Few will even take note of the changes. Instead, they will close their doors and teach as they have always. Why should teachers change unless those changes are related to individual and shared beliefs about what is important in the school?

Keeping the ultimate vision and current mission in mind, curriculum committees must work backwards from the general to the specific. This is like building a house and beginning with an artist's rendering of the dream. Working from the dream, architects, engineers, contractors, and buyers work on the details through floor plans, detailed drawings of how trusses fit together, renderings of electrical and other services, and other fine points until they have planned criteria for selecting the lot.

Even after the lot is selected, plans may change periodically as unexpected conditions affect their implementation. Similarly, even though vision and mission must guide curriculum design and implementation, changing conditions affecting the context for learning may cause adjustments along the way. Testing the curriculum is just as important as designing the curriculum. Administrators must work closely with curriculum design and implementation teams to see that they remain flexible. Teachers cannot be allowed to get hung up on specific materials or texts. Quite frequently the best materials come from the hard work of teachers.

Principals who expect their teachers to be innovative invest in them. Investment includes involvement in professional associations that extends beyond being a dues-paying member, availability of current professional periodicals and books, staff development planning directly related to content and delivery of curriculum, and evaluation of instruction that directly relates to the intended curriculum.

ROLE OF STANDARDS

Lately, it seems, people have developed a positive fascination for learning standards. Adoption of national, state, and district standards are very much in vogue. A persuasive argument for standards is that they set clear expectations that help students perform well (Resnick & Nolan, 1995). In the absence of formal standards, student learning remains a largely undirected activity. Achievement tends to be influenced more by the sequence of teachers experienced by students than the sequence of courses they experience. Written standards set goals and expectations, and they provide a shared understanding of what students should know and be able to do as a result of their schooling.

The American Federation of teachers would like to see standards drive reforms at state level. The AFT believes standards must:

+ focus on academics;

+ be grounded in core disciplines rather than in interdisciplinary outcomes, skills, or understandings;

+ be specific enough to result in a core curriculum (but not to the exclusion of other important elements of education serving advanced students, vocational students, special education students);

+ be manageable given the time constraints under which schools must operate;

+ provide rigorous and world-class challenges comparable to the expectations held for high-achieving students;

+ create a core curriculum suitable for college- and noncollege-bound students; and

+ lead to an appropriate evaluation of student achievement that addresses not only what students should know and be able to do but also how well they should know and be able to perform.

In short, the standards must help parents and educators answer the question of "how good is good enough?" (Gandal, p. 20). In addition, the AFT would like standards to include multiple performance indicators which recognize that not all students will perform at the same levels, yet which stretch all students to their potential. Lifting the bar on "how good is good enough," AFT wants standards to combine knowledge and skills, not dictate how material is taught (i.e., guide, not limit instruction), and be written clearly so that teachers understand what is required of them and their students (Gandal, for AFT, 1995).

Not everyone believes curriculum should be driven by standards. In the same issue of *Educational Leadership* that features AFT's position on standards, Arthur Costa and Rosemarie Liebmann write that content-driven curriculum is passé and that in this fast-changing and knowledge-creating world, process is as important as content. These experts suggest that content-based curriculum fails to teach students to think for themselves. Episodic separation of content from potential application opportunities causes students to associate learning with passing a test rather than as acquiring wisdom and developing personal meaning (Costa & Liebmann, 1995). Content based on traditional ways of thinking is not adequate for future generations who must think creatively and make connections across continuously emerging new content.

Deciding on the role national standards should play is complicated unless you know them well. Standards work at the national level has been completed in the areas of mathematics (thought by many to be the most useable standards), English language arts, science, fine arts, geography, civics and government, and history (thought by some to be the most uneven and least usable standards). Interestingly, development of the standards was itself not standardized. In some cases, professional associations took on the charge without government funding, as did the National Council of Teachers of Mathematics. Other standards, history, for example, emerged from coalitions supported by government grants. So far, all national standards have been proposed as voluntary and designed to serve as guidelines for state and local education officials. Before deciding on the role such standards might play in your local curriculum, obtain copies of them from the U.S. Department of Education, your state education agency, professional associations, or professional publications. Review them carefully. Then decide what role they might play in your classrooms only after carefully comparing them to your definition of curriculum, the role curriculum and teaching will play in the lives of your students, your shared vision of schooling, and your building's shared mission.

State and local educators are simultaneously engaged in standard-setting exercises separate from the work of national curriculum panels. Standards and their cousins, outcomes, are creating a stir with some parent groups who see both as attempts to homogenize and politicize what should be a strictly academic curriculum. Outcomes-based education (OBE) was originally proposed as an innovation that would help American students catch up in international comparisons by focusing on what instruction should produce. The concept was well received by American business, which saw outcomes as a vehicle for clarifying knowledge and skills expectation for ready-to-work employees. At one time, up to 36 states had engaged outcomes as part of the state's approach to learning, accreditation, or assessment. Critics say state-level outcomes are difficult to measure, espouse values better dealt with by parents, and usurp local control. Proponents see outcomes as a means of promoting instructional creativity and interdisciplinary team teaching and learning. They also believe adoption of outcomes will cause schools to abandon Carnegie units (Zlatos, 1993).

States appear to have found the notion of standards less politically volatile than the notion of outcomes. Forty-eight states have developed standards for student achievement. In most cases, schools are not required to use state standards as a framework for local curriculum decisions. However, it is important to note that most states have assessment systems in place that evaluate student performance against those standards. For states that have historically valued local autonomy in educational planning and decision-making, this is an interesting development. Testing programs seem like a back door for ensuring local alignment with curricular decisions that have been made more remotely.

CURRICULUM DELIVERY

Even those who restrict their definition of curriculum to what is taught must be concerned at some point with *how* that content is delivered to students. The "how," in turn, centers on two technologies, that of the teacher and that of the machine. The technology of the teacher involves attitudes (toward students, learning, and schools), knowledge (of how children develop and learn, of content, and of curriculum), investment (in the mission of the school and in personal growth), and skills (instructional and interpersonal). The technology of the machine has to do with the ability of teachers to use technology as a tool to improve the efficiency and effectiveness of students meeting the curriculum.

THE TECHNOLOGY OF THE TEACHER

The relationship between teachers and students is central to learning. Principals need to consider how they can impact the relationships of teachers and students with the school mission, each other, the curriculum, and themselves. Teachers and students who understand and share the school's mission will behave very differently in the classroom than will teachers and students who have no shared understanding of the school's purpose. How well they understand and buy into the school mission determines the types of investment students and teachers have in the classroom. Are they fully focused on achievements that support the school mission? Or does each teacher and student work to achieve a purely personal agenda? Do teachers make an effort to relate their teaching activities to the greater purpose of the school?

The relationship between teachers and students goes a long way toward motivating students to learn. Nearly all students, regardless of their primary motivation, want to be recognized or appreciated. Principals need to examine what type of relationships between teachers and students the culture supports. Are teachers expected to keep their distance and establish strict classroom routines? Are teachers expected to engage in extracurricular and other activities so that students see them in a variety of settings other than the classroom? Are teachers expected to make home visits so that they understand the types of support and challenges students bring with them to school each day? Teachers' attitudes toward students, the school, and the community are displayed in the ways they relate to students. Relationships between teachers and students will vary. But teachers and students should know what type of relationship best upholds the school mission. The extent to which a principal is able to encourage a good working relationship between teachers and students influences the school climate, regardless of whether it is dominated by the need to achieve, affiliate, compete, or be recognized.

The relationship of teachers and students with each other and the extent to which they share the school mission impacts their relationships with the curriculum. Teachers must be knowledgeable about the content, sequence, overlap, and materials of the curriculum. Teachers must also know how children develop physically, emotionally, and intellectually. Good teachers do more than present a curriculum. They dig deep within themselves, their students, and their resources to engage themselves and their students in a meaningful interaction with the curriculum. A teacher's skill in making students active learners who are engaged in meaningful ways with the curriculum makes or breaks the curriculum's effectiveness. No amount of curriculum planning, integration, or alignment will negate the affects of unskilled teaching on students' feelings about the curriculum.

Even those who take a conservative approach to curriculum, viewing curriculum as the content of academic courses, have strong opinions regarding how teachers should present the curriculum. A conservative perspective does not necessarily dictate that every teacher approach the intersection of students and curriculum in the same way. In fact, the most conservative perspective is to have confidence that local hiring practices result in the best qualified teachers being placed in classrooms. If we did an excellent job of hiring, we can be confident our students will be well-instructed, regardless of the particular techniques practiced by the teachers, or so goes conventional wisdom.

In contrast, as definitions of curriculum broaden, approaches to delivery of the curriculum may actually become more prescriptive. A school using behavioral objectives to guide student learning and assessment would be more directive by evaluating teachers based on a particular set of techniques such as those taught by Madeline Hunter. Schools in which the curriculum is considered to be both academic and extracurricular may expect teachers to engage students in competitive activities, make participation in extracurricular activities dependent on classroom performance, and sponsor one or more aspects of the extracurricular program. Schools serious about the systems approach to instruction may insist that delivery of the curriculum involves the use of teacher teams and interdisciplinary student projects.

What goes on in the classroom directly communicates the culture of a school. Valued content gets taught, regardless of the written curriculum. Principals should constantly ask, "How well aligned with the written curriculum is what actually gets taught?" If the similarity is slight, either the "delivered" curriculum (what gets taught), the "intended" curriculum (what is written), or both need to be changed. Valued teaching styles are rewarded by successful students, reflected not only in the grades they receive, but in overall learning and love of learning.

What instructional skills does your school value? Does the school most value teachers who primarily lecture, engage students in cooperative learning, teach facts through experiences, work as part of an interdisciplinary team, or organize learning as part of a collaborative but discipline-based team? What is the role of teaching aides, both human and technical, in the delivery of instruction? In what ways does the definition and delivery of curriculum serve special education students as well as general education students? To what extent and in what ways are teachers of special and general education students expected to work together? Will students be best served by the curriculum in traditional grade level classrooms, ungraded or multiage classrooms, middle school family teams, block schedules, or disciplinary departments? These questions have right answers specific to each local context. The challenge is to work with others to answer these questions for your school in light of its vision, mission, and definition of curriculum.

THE TECHNOLOGY OF THE MACHINE

Educators today cannot responsibly ignore technology, particularly computers, whether they are viewed as either a teaching tool or as an indirect curriculum of their own. For many students, technology plays such an important part in their everyday lives that it has become nearly transparent. Home computers, bank machines, supermarket checkouts, video games, programmable alarm clocks, videotape machines, microwaves, stereos, automated and on-line libraries, farm equipment, and automobiles use computers to service people better. Educators are receiving pressure to integrate use of technology, particularly computers, in delivery of their curricula. A great deal of this pressure arises from the technology industries who create curriculum-related software and easy Internet access. Pressure also comes from potential employers of their graduates and parents, who share concern about their children's future employment opportunities. And don't forget pressure in the form of optional grant money (and what school isn't seeking more funding from just about any source) from the federal government, state government, and various private foundations. Each group pushes for increased technology in the classroom.

Many schools have planned for and encourage technology for delivery of the curriculum. Other schools have allowed technology to creep into their classrooms in predictable but unplanned ways that rely primarily on teacher initiative. Still other schools are struggling with their faculty's ambivalent feelings about technology. According to a 1995 report of Office of Technology Development, most teachers use technology in traditional ways. This includes use of videos for presenting information and computers for basic skills practice and word processing. More sophisticated uses, like desktop publishing, developing higher order reasoning skills through simulations, and the manipulation of databases, are still relatively rare. Overall, it appears that the potential of computers and other technology is underrealized in our schools.

Principals must make sure that their schools plan for the adoption, implementation, and improvement of technology associated with the curriculum and student achievement. To be really effective in managing the curriculum, principals should consider technology both from the perspective of technology as a tool and as its own curriculum. How technology is used in classrooms and extracurricular activities sends a strong message not only about the academic curriculum, but about what we want students to learn from using it.

Several important decisions need to be made about which technologies contribute in what ways to student mastery of the curriculum. Planning for technology involves a basic decision about its role in the school and the role of teachers. Several important steps lead to planning for technology in the curriculum and as curriculum. Begin by building a team who understands the significance of technology in students' lives and its potential for improving efficiency of instruction and student achievement. Such a team may not exist in your school right now, and, frankly, you do not want to rely on only the zealots everyone else has conveniently ignored or isolated. Include skeptics and build team cohesiveness by facilitating the education of all team members before you begin the work of thinking about the role of technology in your school. Expose your team to the possibilities, using faculty and students from other schools, research, and "success story" literature about technology in other schools, futures experts, your own community, and your own students.

Next, revisit the collective vision of what your school should be. Pay particular attention to the hidden and overt roles of technology in that ideal vision. Then work backward from the vision. Remembering our earlier analogy, think of this work like building a house. In this scenario, you are building your dream house. Although you have looked at many other houses, you have never actually seen this house because it is your dream house; no one else has envisioned it or built it. Your vision is like the artist rendering of the dream house. Work backwards from there, putting in the details layer after layer, until you have the criteria for selecting the building site or lot. In the case of technology, the lot becomes the place technology should be located, stored, and used.

Keep your plan flexible. Even when building your dream house you make changes during construction due to unanticipated conditions, materials problems, and building code challenges. Don't get hung up on hardware. When selecting software, keep in mind your curriculum and the goals of efficiency and effectiveness as measured by student achievement.

Important decisions have to be made. Exactly what do you want technology's place to be in student learning? Will you be intentionally teaching skills? Or will skills be acquired through the natural course of teaching content? Is technology to be a transparent learning and teaching tool, or will a particular content be associated with it? What role will the school have in supervising student and staff use of technologies, particularly communication technologies for which you may want to limit access and write acceptable use policies? How will use of technology in elementary schools impact the curriculum elsewhere? For example, a current "hot" question is when and where (even whether) to teach students keyboarding, a skill traditionally reserved to high school typing and word processing classes. How will use of technology at various grades and in various disciplines affect current disciplines, departments, and classes? Will your business department grow, shrink, or cease to exist? Who will own the technology? Traditionally, computers have been under the supervision of particular departments, the library, or separate lab supervisors. Some schools put a small number of computers in each classroom. What is best for your entire school's curriculum?

A fatal flaw is to sink all your funds into hardware, software, and furniture, neglecting "peopleware" in the process. Only by investing in people, perhaps spending up to 30% of what you spent on the "technical" side of the plan, will you achieve your goal of efficient and effective integration of technology as a tool and as an indirect curriculum. Plan also for ongoing support for the hardware, software, and peopleware. One-time installation and training will not lead to effective implementation. Instead, they will lead to discouraged teachers and a retreat to years-old practices with which they are most comfortable. It will lead to obsolete equipment you cannot afford to replace or repair. Your team must find ways to support, evaluate, and continue planning in the face of rapidly changing technologies worldwide (Uebbing, 1995).

EVALUATION OF STUDENTS AND THE CURRICULUM

Later, we devote a full chapter to ways in which effective principals play a role in the evaluation of student learning. However, some preliminary thoughts are appropriate here.

Most likely the curriculum of your school takes into account national (maybe international), state, and local expectations of schools. In the best of all worlds, the curriculum clearly promotes the public and shared mission of your school. Teachers and students understand how what they are doing at each grade level and each discipline matters in terms of the purpose of your school. The principal is responsible for transforming this ideal situation into real circumstances. Two ways to promote such conditions are to link student evaluation to the curriculum and to evaluate the curriculum itself.

Linking evaluation of students to what they are taught does not seem to be a radical idea. Fenwick English (1988), a prominent writer in the field of curriculum, advises schools to develop aligned curricula in which what is taught is what is tested. Schools are advised to first design the curriculum, stressing what children should learn, then design the assessment processes. End-of-chapter tests, which focus on only part of a unit of study, are rarely relevant to broader assessment objectives. Even professionally developed standardized tests are often used to judge how well students are progressing through school without serious examination of the fit between assessment and curriculum.

The principal, the instructional leader, is responsible for seeing that students are assessed on the content of the curriculum they are taught and that they are able to demonstrate expected skills. At the bottom line, the principal must work with teachers to see that students are appropriately assessed on what they are expected to know and be able to do.

This seemingly simple concept is complex to implement. Student assessment techniques may include acceptance of teacher professional judgment, teacher-developed tests, locally developed tests for shared use, standardized tests (sometimes adapted to better fit the local curriculum), or portfolios (folders, notebooks, boxes, and technology- and performance-based assessment before a panel of trained evaluators). Who gets assessed is an important related issue. Will special education students be assessed in the same ways as other students? What about students for whom English is not their first language? However obvious the answer to this question may seem to you, the opposite answer seems as obvious to someone else.

Only a thorough examination of your school's mission and important relationships between teachers, students, and the curriculum can guide decisions about assessment. The principal's role is to see that student assessment is thoughtfully examined in this light and is implemented in ways valuable to the students, teachers, and parents.

Reporting assessment results to parents, the school board, and other members of the public is also a concern of the principal. Even if the superintendent manages the actual reporting, interpreting, and explaining of the assessment process, results and uses of data to inform curriculum content and delivery are the principal's responsibilities.

The curriculum cannot be allowed to become static. Regular inspection of the curriculum serves as a means of quality control and assurance that the curriculum remains in line with current vision, mission, and policies. Even in districts with large central office staff and curriculum specialists, building principals must not neglect curriculum design, delivery, and evaluation. Each principal must constantly ask whether the curriculum being taught is what is intended, and how well that curriculum serves the school's students. Principals should work with faculty and central office, if appropriate, to establish a cycle of curriculum review and revision. The trick to making such a system more than an intellectual paper exercise is to begin with studying the relationship between the written curriculum, the delivered curriculum, and the school mission. Discrepancies in these relationships invalidate any other curriculum planning and must be reconciled before new plans can be made.

REFLECTING ON YOUR SCHOOL'S CURRICULUM

Begin evaluating your school's curriculum and the leadership you provide to curriculum issues by answering the following questions for yourself. If you answer, "I don't know," you should find the answer right away.

- Do we have a long-range plan?
- Do we have policies and practices to assure the development and delivery of a quality curriculum?
- Do I as principal create time in my schedule to focus on quality design and implementation of curriculum?
- What processes are in place to monitor and modify the curriculum and its implementation? What data do we gather to check whether students are learning what is expected?
- How do we use these data?
- Does our budgeting process support our curriculum?
- What support mechanisms are in place to assist teachers in creatively addressing student needs through delivery of the curriculum?
- How do our hiring practices affect design and delivery of the curriculum?
- Do students and their parents know their responsibilities for the curriculum?
- Is the curriculum communicated to external and internal suppliers and customers (from parents to next-level teachers to community to central office)?

- How does our school culture (communicated and living values) and climate (environment for learning) contribute to the design and delivery of curriculum?
- How does the way in which we are organized (grade levels, departments, interdisciplinary teams) contribute to delivery of the curriculum?
- How do we address the needs of students as individuals, both special education and regular education students?
- To what extent is technology a tool for teaching and learning in the academic or core learning areas?
- In what ways is the community involved in design and implementation of the curriculum? Do we deliver a common core to all students or differentiate expectations for students? Why do we do that?
- To what extent do our resources rely upon or go beyond textbooks?
- How much room do we allow for teacher judgment regarding curriculum implementation and supplementation?
- What are our measures of success?
- What can I as principal do to make myself an expert in the curriculum taught in my building?

ELIZABETH HARRIS: MAKING CURRICULUM AN EXPRESSION OF CENTRAL'S MISSION

Central's leadership team was reformed at the beginning of the second year. Half the members left the team and new members were elected. At least, Elizabeth sighed, the leadership team had worked closely with faculty and staff the year before, so making a change in the guiding group was not traumatic. Probably it was healthy. Certainly, the previous year had inspired some people who would once have sat on their hands and their ideas. Now ideas were flying. Elizabeth needed to find a way for the school to harness the energy and the ideas. She sensed this year was crucial. At the end of three years at

Central she needed to show the school moving forward, beyond listing ideas and values.

At midterm of her first year at Central, Elizabeth enlisted the assistance of an external facilitator from a nearby university to help the leadership team identify its role and priorities. The facilitator agreed to continue working with her and the leadership team as an advisor and process observer. He would help plan productive meeting agendas, facilitate decision-making groups, and provide feedback regarding how well people worked together at faculty meetings and leadership group meetings. Together with the reinvented leadership team, they planned a year of work toward critical goals. Elizabeth dreamed of implementing as many of the plans as possible in the second semester of her third year at Central and implementing others throughout her fourth year.

The leadership team decided to study and plan for improvements in curriculum and instruction, teacher empowerment and collaboration, and community partnerships.

Elizabeth took particular interest in this ad hoc curriculum and instruction study and planning team. During her first two years at Central, the elected Curriculum Committee, a holdover from the previous administration, had been a desirable committee because it didn't meet very often. The lack of meetings reflected the lack of business. The only activity of the Curriculum Committee had been to approve the addition of a course on business technology and an advanced placement world history class. The Curriculum Committee did not see critical study of the curriculum as within its purview. Curriculum began at the department level and, in the committee's mind, the department level is where it ended. The function of the Curriculum Committee was simply to make sure that no department overstepped its bounds by proposing to add a course that would overlap or conflict with a course offered by another department. In essence, the Curriculum Committee had become guardian of the status quo.

The regular Curriculum Committee continued to function in its fashion as the leadership team's ad hoc curriculum and instruction study group went to work. At its first meeting, the curriculum and instruction study group engaged in a long consideration of just what it should do. The group discussed the importance of encouraging innovation while maintaining quality.

The curriculum and instruction study group finally decided its work would be to develop processes through which Central could create, model, and evaluate innovative curriculum, teaching, and learning strategies. Convinced by the prior year's experiences that good data help make good decisions, the group surveyed faculty, staff, parents, and students regarding the importance of certain skills and content. The group also studied course outlines and interviewed faculty, looking for clear expectations of students and alignment of courses in curricular areas from year to year.

The committee's findings were somewhat surprising. Central's formal and informal curriculum shared certain similarities. Nevertheless, the proprietary nature of some courses, which had "belonged" to particular faculty for several years, had resulted in very idiosyncratic approaches to the curriculum. Likewise, turnover in some departments without mentoring of new faculty by those who preceded them had resulted in delivery of course content that, in some cases, looked very different from the written curriculum. Often, it was more desirable than what appeared in the curriculum notebooks collecting dust on department chairs' shelves.

But alignment was clearly out of whack. In a few cases, such as in the math department, the sequence of courses and expectations for student performance in those courses was very clear. It was less clear in other departments, such as English, where faculty had turned over significantly during the past five years and in which juniors and seniors had several courses from which to choose. Faculty, parents, and students rated problem solving and decision making as priority skills that could be addressed by the curriculum. At the same time, faculty rated addressing the needs of an increasingly diverse student population even higher.

The committee came face-to-face with issues of student assessment. Declining SAT scores were not what they seemed at first. Ten years ago only about 60% of Central's students actually expected to attend college, and only those students took the SAT. More recently, nearly every Central student expected to attend college. Nearly 75% of the students intended to attend a four-year college immediately following high school. Most of the rest expected to enroll either full- or part-time at a nearby community college. In preparing for their highest expectations, more than 90% of Central's students had come to take the SAT. In fact, counselors at the school encouraged students to do so. Declining scores appeared more reflective of the increasing expectations of test takers than of poor preparation.

The curriculum and instruction study committee used the local university and its own Internet connections to explore options that would allow Central to align curriculum, address the diverse needs of learners, test what is taught, and report with some confidence on the academic progress of Central students. In the past, individual departments had done this type of work, with little or no collaboration among departments. The study committee examined the standards movement and came to the conclusion that, in some ways, the standards movement faced the same challenges of isolation. A few teachers argued, however, that interdisciplinary standards led to watered down requirements and affective outcomes, which they wanted to avoid.

Related to the issue of standards were concerns about student assessment. Current literature promoted the use of performance assessments and student portfolios. Some teachers found these ideas attractive alternatives to traditional testing approaches. Others suspected these new approaches to assessment would be too weak and subjective. Stacks of journal articles supporting and criticizing alternative assessments were copied and shared by those on both sides of the argument.

By April of Elizabeth's second year at Central, the curriculum and instruction study group brought recommendations before the entire faculty and staff. They reminded everyone that they had worked hard to keep the mission of Central in mind at all stages of exploring curriculum and assessment issues. They felt their final recommendations especially reflected the mission's focus on educating young people for work and higher education and the values of diversity, equity, individualism, and collaboration. Their recommendations were:

- ◆ to experiment with standard-setting and alternative assessments within and across disciplines by establishing a team-taught program for English, math, science, and social studies at the freshman level;

- to reinvent an advisor-advisee program that had once served students well but had more recently fallen into disuse;

- to develop a technology plan, including funding sources, to integrate technology across the disciplines;

- to work with community resources to develop a tech prep program for college- and noncollege-bound students;

- to establish a curriculum audit system that would work with teachers at the department level to evaluate and revise both the intended and the delivered curriculum on a predictable schedule; and

- to work with other high schools and the central office to publish an annual report regarding student achievements inside and outside the classroom that would include explanations of the ways in which students were accepting challenges they might once have avoided, such as the SAT.

6

WORKING WITH, SUPPORTING, AND SUPERVISING STAFF

Current leadership literature practically bubbles over with words like teamwork, collaboration, and facilitation. Gone, say many authors, are the days of heavy-handed, top-down management. Flatten the hierarchy, communicate through a web not a chain, and *coach* employees to higher performance. At the same time, the clamor for accountability translates into holding teachers responsible for student achievement of high academic standards. Most states have legislated requirements regarding principals' responsibilities for evaluating teachers. However, evaluation of teachers is negotiable with the union in many districts. Principals must find ways to make sense of these conflicting mandates. Nowhere is the role of the principal more confused than in the carefully forged relationships principals must build to work with, support, and supervise other adults in the building.

WORKING WITH TEACHERS AND OTHER STAFF

The ability to work with other adults in a school building is not so different from working with children. Good working relationships require genuine belief in the meanings of two little words: trust and respect.

TRUST

Trust is a two-way street that principals must pave. Principals must establish conditions under which it possible for staff to trust them. Most veteran teachers and other staff members have seen administrators at all levels come and go. Many have had experiences that cause them to become aggressive about their needs or to avoid the principal unless an encounter is absolutely necessary. This legacy greets new principals and takes years to dispel. At the same time, the ways in which superintendents and principals interact do not always model collaboration and mutual confidence. This makes the building of the trusting two-way street an even greater challenge.

How do you build trust? Just think for a moment about the one or two people whom you trust completely. They probably behave predictably, love you even when you are wrong, always tell you the truth (kindly), listen to you even when you don't expect a response, respect your confidentiality, provide expert assistance, and never overstep their bounds.

Translate what we know about the trustworthiness of good friends to the principalship. It is not necessary, and may not be desirable, to become good friends with all your teachers. However, when it comes to trustworthiness, principals should exhibit behaviors of good friends.

First, be predictable. If you are consistent in sharing your educational philosophy, working toward fulfillment of a vision of what the school can be, and making decisions in keeping with the school mission, you are probably trustworthy. If people know what you stand for and that certain words and actions are unacceptable to you, you are probably trustworthy. On the other hand, if your decisions reflect personal influence, fad, or opportunity, you are unpredictable. If you ignore behavior in one person that angers you in another, you are unpredictable. If five people give different versions of what they believe is important to you, you are unpredictable. Predictability as a facilitator of trust does not require that everyone agree with you. It does require that everyone know what you believe and that you will make decisions based on the publicly held values of the school as expressed through the mission.

Supporting and supervising staff in any meaningful way is impossible without trust. Support that is present one day but withdrawn the next is harmful and divisive. To be trustworthy, you must be predictable when you promise to support an idea or deed. Supervision that is no more than a routine checking off of behaviors or characteristics is a waste of your and the teachers' time. Teachers must be able to believe you will tell them the truth, make a sincere effort to provide them the resources they need to be better, and maintain the confidentiality of their evaluations.

People who love you unconditionally are trustworthy. Unconditional love doesn't mean always approving of what others do. Unconditional love doesn't mean ignoring mistakes. Unconditional love doesn't mean tolerating rudeness or poor performance. However, principals can support teachers who take well-conceived risks to improve instruction, student achievement, or other worthy goals that align with the school mission. Unconditional acceptance means not punishing innovators when their schemes go awry. It means giving them opportunities to innovate again. It also means picking innovators up when they fall, reminding them of what they did right, and urging them to try again.

People who are trustworthy tell you the truth. Always. Principals who want trust must be truthful with faculty and staff. The truth may be delivered in very different ways, depending on the people involved, the circumstances, and the need for sensitivity. Nonetheless, a trustworthy principal tells the truth. Telling the truth does not require telling everything you know. It may sometimes require saying, "I cannot share that information," or, "I'm not comfortable discussing it with you at this time." If you are known for telling the truth, your staff will believe you when you tell them that they did a good job or that they deserve community recognition for their efforts. A reputation for being truthful also motivates staff to perform highly when asked to do special projects you say will benefit students. Telling the truth requires modesty, for it demands not exaggerating your knowledge or importance around the building or in other arenas. Being truthful is part of being predictable. People who work with you should be able to predict that you will tell them the truth.

Trustworthy people are good listeners who respect people's confidentiality. Morris and other researchers (1981) found that urban principals spent 80% of each day in face-to-face interactions with staff, students, and others. Good interpersonal skills are essential. At the top of the list is being a good listener.

A trustworthy listener listens for understanding. Someone who listens for understanding can be trusted to set aside personal biases. Listening for understanding also means momentarily abandoning a personal agenda for that of the speaker. To mentally plan your next activity while a teacher describes a student's behavior is not characteristic of a good listener. Listening for understanding allows a speaker to finish the story. To interrupt with questions, judgments, or solutions invites the conversation to become longer, not shorter. Part of understanding the speaker is to understand the speaker's need to explain, complain, or justify. After the story is told, the good listener asks clarifying questions before recommending solutions.

A good listener also is aware of the effects habitual responses have on listeners. For example, studies of male and female communication patterns suggest that men and women listen quite differently. Men interrupt more, perhaps because they are eager to get to the facts and identify a solution quickly. Women are more likely to encourage the speaker to share feelings and details. Women are less likely to interrupt and more likely to express support. Men are not necessarily less supportive, but they do not feel the need to affirm their support. (Rudman, 1996). Part of being trustworthy is practicing gender- and culture-neutral responses and adapting physical and verbal responses to each speaker so that listeners won't misinterpret you.

Trustworthy listeners respect confidentiality. Maintaining confidentiality certainly requires protection of sensitive information identified by law, personal rules, and student file regulations. However, being trustworthy requires practicing confidentiality at other levels. Trust is built at the interpersonal level by not sharing amusing, exasperating, or interesting conversations with others, no matter how tempting. Others may repeat the conversations or be influenced in their attitudes toward someone else because of the conversation. Administrators who must blow off steam may discuss incidents with other administrators they trust to keep the confidence or with spouses. A wise administrator who wants to remain trustworthy cautions the spouse that whatever is shared at home must remain there. Many communities treat words coming from the mouth of a principal's spouse as if they came from the principal. Being trustworthy as a listener requires that conversations be publicly told only by the other party, not by the principal or principal's confidant.

Trustworthy people provide expert assistance. Principals who can be trusted provide expertise in general school law, school policies and rules, student management, and other areas of daily school life. Most important to being trustworthy in working with, supporting, and supervising teachers is expertise in teaching and learning. The extent of a principal's trustworthiness as a staff developer, classroom coach, or teacher evaluator is directly proportional to staff perceptions of the principal's level of understanding. Trustworthy principals never stop learning about curriculum and instruction. They read professional journals about what should happen in the classroom, and they share what they read with teachers

Trustworthy people don't overstep their bounds. Principals become trustworthy by establishing clear limits to relationships with teachers and other staff members. Others who work in the school must believe the principal cares about them and plays no favorites. Resources must be equitably distributed. Communication must be open with all staff members. Secret deals cannot be part of the principal's administrative style. Staying in bounds also means not expecting teachers and other staff members to be the principal's best friends, not sharing personal opinions and problems, and limiting involvement in staff members' personal lives. Knowing boundaries does not mean being cold and impersonal. Being trustworthy does mean establishing consistent limits to personal relationships associated with professional work.

RESPECT

Mutual respect, a close relative of trust, is essential to working productively with others. The changing nature of the principalship requires facilitating groups, engaging other adults in decision-making roles with which they may not be initially comfortable, and motivating teachers to take risks. For the principal to *work with* people rather than *dictate to* people, other adults in the building must respect the principal as an authority. This is not as contradictory as it may seem at first glance. Teachers must respect the principal's accountability for everything associated with the school, from learning to locking. Teachers must also respect that the principal's career is determined, in part, by the types of decisions and products made in the building.

In the beginning, respect comes with the position. But positional authority fades with time. Lasting respect, respect for expertise and interpersonal savvy, is earned, not inherited. The principal's actions, more than words, gain respect from teachers, staff, parents, students, central office, community members, and others. This type of respect links directly to the principal's ability to "walk the talk" of personal educational philosophy, school vision, and school mission. Making decisions in light of the school mission and educating others about the reasons for those decisions lead to lasting respect. Communicating the how and why of decisions, not just assuming everyone either already understands or is uninterested, is important to building a track record of consistency and respect. Regardless of the subject, conversations can become opportunities to demonstrate regard for the professional judgments and feelings of others. Honoring others reflects positively on the principal. In short, respect is earned in proportion to the amount given.

The other side of the respect issue is the principal's level of esteem for others who work in the school. Respect for other adults in the school starts with recognition of their contributions and experiences. Regardless of whatever formal or informal evaluations each has received, every member of the school organization has given something of value to the school. Each has given something of himself or herself. Circumstances may have caused an individual's dedication to fade. Find out each person's history with the school. Respecting individual, historic contributions may be a first step in re-igniting spent passions. Find ways, even by appointment, to engage people in conversations regarding the school, their work, and their needs. If these conversations take place in an atmosphere of trust, they will likely reveal information, ideas, history, talents, and motivations previously unknown, even to some seasoned administrators. Respecting each adult's story and any efforts made to capitalize on the stories in positive ways will be reflected in mutual respect and support for the principal.

The principal's actions cultivate respect. Remember your grandmother's admonition that actions speak louder than words? Remember also earlier parts of this book where we pointed out that what you do is the most reliable expression of what you value? If you want the respect of teachers and other staff members, your actions must show that you value them. Demonstrate respect by addressing each in front of students as

"Mr.," "Miss," "Mrs.," and "Ms." If applicable, use titles such as "Dr." Speak to teachers in front of students in friendly and respectful ways. Do not disparage others, students or adults, in front of other students or adults. Use your office, a conference room, corner, or other location away from the ears of others to correct behaviors. Recognize large and small successes through public congratulations in the halls, work areas, and lunch areas. Write notes about things well done. Show respect for the entire group of adults with whom you work by bringing in food or other small treats. These are not sappy acts designed to make you look like a nice person. These are accepted means in most schools of demonstrating your respect for the other adults who work with the children whose education is at the center of your reason for being in the school.

Respect is more than restraining from public criticism and practicing public praise. Other actions speak even louder. The ultimate expression of respect is *empowerment*. Empowering the adults in your school entails using them as resources you trust to make professional decisions about important aspects of the school. Empowerment is not an overnight phenomenon. Empowerment results from extensive investment in teamwork skills and knowledge of effective and innovative practices. Staff empowerment through study groups, task forces, committees, and teaching teams not only increases buy-in of the people who have to do the work in decisions. It also increases respect for the administrator whose use of these work groups communicates respect for others.

SUPPORTING OTHERS THROUGH TEAM BUILDING

Supporting others involves several skills, beginning with trust and respect, expressed through two primary mechanisms: building a sense of team and staff development.

A team cannot exist for long without endorsement of the organization's leader. At the same time, investment solely in individuals without attention to the importance of creating a team of adults who work toward a shared vision and mission will result in a stagnant school. The interactions of the adults who work in the school are critical to the school's effectiveness. Peters and Waterman (1984), in *In Search of Excellence*, note that groups, not individuals, are the building blocks of excellent organizations. Even in schools where classroom doors close easily, it is becoming increasingly difficult to operate that way. Part of the principal's job of supporting staff is to find ways in which to encourage staff to work as members of the group. If we examine the informal ways in which school employees organize, we find that most are members of one or more groups, which influence their behaviors and attitudes. Harnessing the power of groups is a supporting activity.

Creating a sense of team in a school building is not easy. Making the effort to do so expresses value for open communication, a wide variety of perspectives, and efforts of groups. These values may run counter to an individualistic culture and past practices. A few individuals may be used to getting all their recognition, rewards, and support from the principal's office. Changing to a supportive culture in which the principal is one means of support requires several steps:

- developing mutual respect,
- sharing a purpose,
- developing supportive rituals,
- finding means for expressions of dissent, and
- becoming more productive as a team than as a collection of individuals.

Mutual respect requires some degree of familiarity. Except in schools that are very affiliative, adults in the building tend to separate into distinct groups. Teachers interact only at certain grade levels, within certain subjects, during certain planning periods, or around certain experiences with the school. Staff likewise create a sort of hierarchy of those who work in the main office, out of maintenance closets, or on the playground. Few people are truly familiar with the personal and professional values of those outside their informally defined groups.

To create team, the principal must create opportunities for increased familiarity. Faculty meetings can include all who work in the school and begin with exercises designed to increase familiarity and shared values. Examples of such exercises include games illustrating advantages of collaboration over competition, group problem-solving exercises, and warmup activities. The agenda of every faculty meeting has room for warmup activities. These short activities help people understand others. For example, ask people to take a coin from their pockets and relate a significant event in their lives from that year. Ask people to describe the most significant educational experience in their lives. Ask people to share something they read or saw in the news during the past week that might have an impact on education. The value of warmups occurs in debriefing or summarizing what people learned both about the subject at hand and about the group. Over time, this increased understanding leads to respect and trust. Libraries and professional associations are great resources for warmups and other games to increase familiarity. Using staff meetings for these activities may, in the long run, be more productive than using them to share information everyone could otherwise read.

We would like to assume that everyone in our schools shares a common purpose. A well-articulated school mission is the most effective mechanism for making this so. As we discussed earlier, maintaining a vision of what a school can be and basing decisions on the school's mission provides staff with reasons for doing what they do. A sense of team is created when both individuals and groups understand how they contribute to success of the mission. Abolish committees that take up time but don't contribute to achieving the mission. Permanent and ad hoc decision-making and planning groups that contribute to achieving the mission should replace them.

High-performing teams rely on supportive rituals to guide their work. Supportive rituals are practices that make the team's work more productive. For example, a staff meeting might always consist of a staff-directed warmup, an in-basket problem-solving session in which one or more members of the staff seek a variety of approaches to a challenge faced on the job, news too important to share in writing, and a closing, inspirational message. A support group formed to deal with special problems of students might always begin with a warmup, followed by presentation of today's problem(s), structured brainstorming, group consensus building, and final words from all members of the support group. Expectations for work between meetings and preprinted agendas may also be part of a team's supporting rituals. As you can see from the examples, supporting rituals vary from school to school and team to team.

Every team has dissenting voices and every one of us from time to time disagrees with team decisions. A healthy team finds nondestructive means by which members may dissent.

The first step in honoring diverse perspectives is to hear them all. This requires both regulating some aggressive public speakers and encouraging the quieter ones. Failure to get all opinions on the table will likely result either in a lower quality decision or limited support for the decision.

Books on group and team facilitation list many mechanisms for managing discussion. One mechanism is to provide each speaker with poker chips or another token symbolizing a minute of speech. Tokens may not be given to or accepted from others. Everyone must use at least one token during the conversation. Another mechanism is to ask each team member (or group of team members) to represent a particular point of view and present it in a limited time. The team leader may also make an effort to call on each member of the team. Assigning a group member to record the time, subjects, and number of times speaking for each group member and asking the observer to share that information with the team at the end of the meeting can also be effective. Regardless of the mechanism, it is important to hear each voice. Many experts on team work recommend that once all voices are heard, consensus be used to reach a decision rather than voting. Voting, although democratic and sometimes necessary because of the nature of decisions, can also be divisive, because it creates winners and losers of record. The purpose of consensus is to reach a decision with which everyone can live.

Team "happens" when the team becomes visibly more productive than a collection of individuals. Sports analogies, such as basketball, which require team members to have both specialized and overlapping skills, come quickly to mind along with academic competitions such as scholastic bowls, debate teams, and computer teams.

Perhaps "experiential learning" serves as a better metaphor for how productive adults can be as school teams. When learning by experience, teams of students in laboratories, at computers, in libraries, at work sites, and elsewhere work together to solve academic problems. The students must analyze the problems, gather resources, develop and test hypotheses, investigate resources, and propose solutions. They must justify their decisions with theories, facts, and logic. Teams of adults who do the same not only perform more productively as a group than they would as individuals. They also model for stu-

dents the significance of the very processes they are expected
to learn.

SUPPORTING OTHERS THROUGH STAFF DEVELOPMENT

Effective staff development concentrates simultaneously
on the needs of individuals, the needs of the school team, the
school's mission, and the shared vision of what is possible and
desirable. Despite more than a decade of innovative work in
the field of staff development, for many the term unfortunately
inspires images of boring and irrelevant "sit and git" sessions.
Staff development's unpopular reputation is the result of both
poorly managed "county institute" type in-service activities
and its more recent association with reform. The solution to
bad schools, poor student test scores, and Johnny's reading
problem was to "fix" teachers by in-servicing them. Principals
can greatly improve staff development simply by recalling the
reasons they dreaded certain staff development activities. The
final step is to make sure they never subject their staff members
to the same tortures.

As school improvement becomes an increasingly build-
ing-based activity, so does the principal's role in using staff development as a mechanism for supporting professionalism. Six
models of staff development emerged during the 1980s: individually guided, observation and assessment, peer coaching,
problem solving, training, and inquiry.

Individually guided staff development promotes learning by
individuals. This model assumes that adults learn best when
they initiate and plan what they are to learn and how they are
to learn it. On the downside, individualization may lead to unnecessary reinvention of the wheel. A second model, *observation and assessment*, provides feedback regarding how well a job
is being done and how to improve it. The model assumes that
feedback and reflection enhance performance. Unfortunately,
this model is too often associated with the unpleasantness that
evaluation connotes. *Peer coaching* may avoid this connection.
Involvement in a school improvement or development process
that requires participants to *solve a problem* is another form of
development. For team members to solve the problem, they
must study resources and collect data. This model assumes that
adults learn most effectively when they have a need to know
something. *Training* is a more traditional model. It is often asso-

ciated with workshops designed primarily to promote awareness or increase knowledge. This model assumes that certain
behaviors and techniques are desirable and that adults can
change their behaviors. *Inquiry* as an approach to staff development enables individuals and groups to study issues that grow
out of their work. This model is based on the belief that teachers
are capable of formulating and pursuing answers to their own
questions of practice (Sparks & Loucks-Horsley, 1989).

Decisions about staff development, like all other decisions,
must directly relate to the school's mission and vision. Inherent
in the relationship between staff development and school improvement is the assumption that both teachers and nonteachers who work in the learning business must themselves continually learn. Inevitably this attractive assumption gives way
to principals complaining that the adults in the school are
much more challenging students than the children. In an interview for a newsletter of the Regional Laboratory for Educational Improvement of the Northeast and Islands, Michael Huberman explains his research on the teacher life cycle. He
reports that at some point in their late 30s or early 40s most
teachers become disengaged, pull back, and build little walls
around their classrooms and themselves. Conversely, more
changes take place in a teacher's first six years of practice than
at any other time in a career (Regional Lab Reports, 1992). Ken-
neth Leithwood (1990) adds that teachers' professional expertise stabilizes in mid-career because of a lack of stimulation
caused by organizational structures and stifling staff development. What can principals do so that staff development serves
all staff, not just the initiates, furthers the school mission, and
increases teacher engagement in the school?

Principals must not present staff development in a single
format. Instead, staff development must form a carefully woven web of activities that overlap and support improved services to students and their parents. Effective staff development
addresses needs of individuals, various groups, and the organization. Staff development must take place in the schoolhouse,
at other schoolhouses, at professional conferences, in the community, and through graduate and continuing education.

This list doesn't imply that staff development is a smorgas-
bord of activities from which teachers and others in the school
may choose to partake or not. To be effective, staff development

must relate to the very core of the school, the school's business, and the classrooms. If it is unrelated, it is unnecessary. If it is truly related, it will be messy, controversial, and filled with challenges regardless of how well-planned the activities.

For principals to lead staff development effectively, they must be clear about its purposes. Occasionally, principals may be able to accommodate the full range of staff development needs, from individual to institutional. Limited resources more often mean that choices must be made.

Inside needs and outside pressures help decide the ways in which a school engages in staff development. Keys to inside needs are individual and collective strengths of the staff and individual and collective needs of the students in relationship to the school's mission. Outside needs come from district offices, state departments, legislatures, funders, and other sources of influence external to the school. For the most part, outside needs appear on the surface to have little relationship to the school's mission. The principal's skill is in finding ways in which to use limited resources to leverage external mandates so that they serve internal needs.

Staff development is like other aspects of the principalship in that actions do the talking. Roland Barth holds that the schoolhouse is the most powerful context for professional development (Barth 1990). Being opportunistic within the framework of the school's mission enables principals to address a wide variety of individual, group, and organizational staff development needs.

An opportunistic principal will seek ways to leverage an outside need (often accompanied by funding) to serve an internal purpose. For example, how could a state mandate to develop local standards for student performance be transformed from an odious task into a learning opportunity for teaching teams? How could this work be structured so that it excites teachers about new approaches to working with students and advances the school mission? What external resources and opportunities for individuals and small groups to visit other schools or attend professional meetings could emerge from the need to complete this activity successfully? An opportunistic principal is flexible and understands when to be a motivational cheerleader, questioning coach, expert advisor, or resource provider (Killion, Huddleston, & Claspell, 1989).

Opportunism and flexibility also allow principals to promote a variety of staff development activities appropriate for
growth stages and motivational needs of staff. Subtle means of
influence include informing teachers of professional opportunities, disseminating professional reading materials, focusing
on a specific theme, soliciting staff opinions, encouraging ex-
perimentation, and recognizing achievements (McEvoy, 1987).
Less subtle approaches to staff development include linking
staff development to teacher evaluation and changing the conditions under which teachers work.

Linking staff development to teacher evaluation can be
tricky, but it can be done. Too often, formal evaluation of teachers fails to fulfill its most important purpose: improvement of
teaching (Barth, 1981). One way to handle this usually uncomfortable task is to view teacher evaluation as an opportunity for
needs assessment. Principals who spend a great deal of time in
classrooms may begin to notice patterns of teaching practices
that could legitimately form the basis of staff development pro-
gramming. Formal charting of observations of classroom instruction and postobservation conversations with teachers
could identify staff development themes and strategies
(Kachur, Goodall, & Ashby, 1990).

Changing the conditions under which teachers work is related to making changes in climate and culture. Making it safe
to take risks changes the conditions under which teachers
work. Teachers who feel safe are more likely to invest in nontraditional staff development opportunities such as study
groups, peer coaching, or team problem solving. Changing the
purpose of faculty meetings from information to ongoing conversations about what happens in classrooms also changes the
conditions of work. Another example of changing the conditions under which teachers work is to rearrange the schedule
so that teachers have time to meet, converse, and train on a
monthly basis for two or more hours at a time. Changing the
ways in which decisions are made about scheduling students,
text selection, or classroom use opens avenues for staff development. Another possibility is to make the curriculum a visible
rather than a private enterprise. Barth (1981) reports that he
once posted teacher curriculum outlines in the faculty room
that revealed what teachers expected to teach rather than what
the official curriculum guidelines required be taught. The pub-

lic posting of the real curriculum exposed overlaps and gaps in what students were learning. Making the real curriculum public changed the conditions under which teachers worked. In like fashion, using the budget to buy books for teachers to read, to have time together outside the classroom but inside normal school hours, to visit other schools, to spend time in the community, to present at professional conferences, and to support graduate education changes the conditions under which teachers work and reinforces the value of staff development.

SUPERVISING STAFF

The thought of being evaluated makes most teachers either shrug ("It's meaningless") or panic ("I get nervous when the principal's in the room"). Many principals have similar reactions. Shrugs mean, "I must do this to be in compliance with the contract but I know it won't make any difference and I wish I could spend my time on something more useful." Panic may mean, "I really want to make a difference, get to every classroom, make insightful comments for which the teachers will respect me, but I'm not sure I really know enough to pull it off." Some principals recognize evaluation day as an opportunity to become familiar with the classroom. Even if they will have little impact, at least they will be knowledgeable when questions about the classroom arise. A few manage to make it a learning occasion for both themselves and teachers. Still fewer use the moment to inform staff development needs.

Communicating high expectations to students and staff sets the tone of supervision. Constantly keeping the mission of the school before the entire school and expressing belief in the ability of all players to contribute to its accomplishment is a means of indirect supervision. By constantly comparing performance, products, and decisions to the mission, the principal communicates the standards to which all members of the school workforce will be held.

Supervising teachers goes well beyond the required formal observation. Supervising instruction requires spending time working directly with teachers on instruction. To be skilled at doing so, principals must use graduate school preparation, professional associations, and other resources to remain current regarding effective instructional practices. They must also study child growth and development and practice exceptional interpersonal skills. Principals must also be fast and willing learners who acquire as much or more from their teachers as they are able to give. Principals must even be willing to "perform" for others by modeling exemplary or experimental teaching techniques or serving as an occasional substitute teacher.

For supervision to serve more than an evaluative moment, the principal must serve as a mentor and prepare other teachers to serve as mentors. The culture must accept the mentoring arrangement as good for teachers and students, so the risk by both mentor and protégé must be rewarded. Mentoring as first described by Homer involves an older sage (Mentor) and a young student (Odysseus). However, among educators age may be a less important factor than experience (Ashby, 1991). Mentors serve several purposes, including:

♦ sharing stories that serve as examples of ways in which protégés might approach similar situations;

♦ active listening and reality checks;

♦ modeling exemplary practices, prodding protégés toward accomplishing goals; and

♦ supporting with words of assurance, access to networks, and exposure to professional resources (Ashby, 1991).

The subject of supervision as an evaluative activity cannot be avoided. Most evaluation requirements include one or more observations of the classroom. Before visiting the classroom, principals should be sure that they and the faculty share an understanding of the evaluation requirements and purposes. The National Association of Secondary School Principals (NASSP) recommends that several informal observations precede the one that goes on record to make the event less stressful. NASSP also makes several other useful recommendations in keeping with the much practiced clinical supervision model of teacher evaluation. The traditional clinical supervision model focuses on teacher classroom behaviors. Principals using this model meet with each teacher before observing a lesson (preconference), observe a class, and meet with each teacher after the lesson (postobservation). According to NASSP, principals should use the preconference to obtain seating charts or other materials that might be helpful and informative. On observation day, principals should arrive before class to observe routines that precede instruction. Principals should not interrupt their observations except in an emergency. All attention should focus on the teacher and the learning environment. Principals should stay for the entire class. Following the clinical supervision model, NASSP urges principals to deliver written observations and evaluations in person, as part of a postobservation debriefing, within 48 hours of the visit (Zepeda, 1995).

The clinical supervision model focuses on what teachers do in the classroom. Because most schools adopt a standardized form for recording and reporting purposes, the principals usually end up trying to meet both the district's needs and the teacher's needs in a single preconference, observation, postobservation sequence. The principal may look for and discuss with each teacher behaviors or activities the teacher identified as of interest. At the same time, the principal is looking for and making judgments about a list of behaviors that all teachers should exhibit.

The clinical supervision model is practical and efficient. It provides teachers with opportunities to discuss their craft with their principal. At its best, the clinical supervision model enables principals and teachers to discuss not only what teachers do, but why they do it. Just as effective principals think differently than do less effective principals, so effective teachers probably have different ways of thinking about the hundreds of interactions they have with students and curriculum each day.

Getting into teachers' heads and helping their thinking mature is the goal behind some schools' efforts to go beyond the ritual rut into which clinical supervision has fallen. "One-size-fits-all" evaluation systems paint a veneer of fairness for critics and contracts. They serve principals well in the rare instance that teacher dismissal is necessary and possible. However, such a system does not take into account different stages of teacher job maturity, differing needs of students, or curricular and instructional innovations.

Only a differentiated evaluation system can simultaneously meet the needs of teachers and accountability. A differentiated system allows teachers, with approval of the principal, to select from several evaluation plans. Together the plans form a system for teacher evaluation. Each plan must have clear goals, strategies, and criteria for success. For example, teachers who lack experience in a certain type of classroom may be required to participate in a structured plan in which the principal provides regular formative feedback in the clinical supervision tradition. Teachers who want support from more experienced colleagues may ask to work with mentors. More experienced teachers may engage in a collegial arrangement in which they work together on materials, strategies, observations, and feedback. Seasoned, self-directed teachers could work with the principal to develop a personalized plan for growth that combines new learning with application at the classroom or school level. Teachers whose performance indicates serious problems may be required to follow a strict improvement plan. This plan may include specific assistance by a teaching team and the principal (Edwards, 1995).

An even more flexible approach to differentiated teacher evaluation involves the use of teaching portfolios. This innovation in teacher evaluation may be inspired in part by new ideas regarding student assessment and practices of the National Board for Professional Teaching Standards. Both beginning and experienced teachers can benefit from collecting artifacts that document their teaching year. Portfolio contents may be strictly prescribed or may be adapted to serve the needs of different types of teachers and their students. Selecting and sharing artifacts with other teachers and with principals provides opportunities for personal reflection and professionally-focused discussions.

Both school improvement literature and legislation regard teacher evaluation as important. Evaluation of other staff receives less discussion. Support staff may be categorized as professional (e.g., librarians, psychologists) and noncertified (e.g., secretaries, custodians, food service workers). Evaluation of professional and noncertified support staff varies from state to state and district to district. In some cases, professional staff must be evaluated using the same models and instruments as used with teachers. In other cases, evaluation of professional staff either requires its own model or relies on the approach used with noncertified staff.

Principals generally acknowledge the importance of a good secretary. People whose jobs include meeting and greeting the public wield a great deal of informal influence. Librarians directly work with children every day. Even so, support staff evaluation generally takes a back seat to other responsibilities. This happens in part because their evaluations are less likely to be required by law. In many cases, support staff evaluations are not part of a contract and so conveniently sit on the back burner. In other cases, support staff evaluations are so tightly prescribed by agreement that principals feel they serve little purpose.

Support personnel generally see themselves as integral to the work of the school. They may even see themselves as part of the administration. Evaluation should build upon these perceptions and open communication. Support staff deserve a predictable and honest evaluation as much as teachers do. For this to happen, principals must approach support staff evaluation the way they approach teacher evaluation. Principals need to understand the jobs of support staff. Job descriptions must remain up-to-date.

Prepare for evaluations at the beginning of each year or during the summer before by asking staff to discuss their jobs with you. Note the activities in which they engage. Then discuss reasons those activities differ from the job descriptions. In some cases, the job descriptions may need revision. In other cases, staff may need to be reminded of their range of responsibilities. Principals should discuss expectations and progress informally many times before formal evaluation, just as they visit classrooms several times before formally evaluating teachers.

Schools have support staff because they are necessary to providing service to children. They are essential to establishing a school climate supportive of student learning. Designing an approach to support staff evaluation should take into account their importance to students. An evaluation model should include:

♦ the needs being met by the position;
♦ specific duties;
♦ performance indicators and standards;
♦ documentation;
♦ evaluation; and
♦ improvement strategies (Stronge & Tucker, 1995).

Principals generally want to find ways to make teacher and staff evaluation painless at least and helpful at best. Before embarking on ambitious designs aimed at improving teacher and staff professionalism, principals must do their legal homework. They must be knowledgeable of and strictly adhere to procedures established by their states, school boards, and negotiated agreements for teacher evaluation. School law classes usually reinforce this notion by citing cases in which poor teachers were reinstated because of procedural error. If staff members consistently perform unsatisfactorily and must be dismissed, principals become the front line in bearing the burden of proof.

Principals can help themselves, teachers, and staff through the inevitable stress of evaluation by focusing on work performance and professional issues. Principals should avoid personal comments and resist the temptation to use the evaluation conference to clear the air about things that bother them. Comments should be concrete so that the ways in which performance can change are clear. The evaluation conference should be an opportunity to discuss both positive and negative aspects of performance. Limit discussion to current issues. The past should stay buried unless it is unquestionably relevant. Nothing should come as a surprise to the employee. The evaluation conference is not an opportunity to ambush employees. Every employee deserves an opportunity during the conference to ask questions and make comments about the job and about the evaluation (Hartzell, 1995).

Principals must keep in mind the purpose of supervision. If the primary purpose is professional growth, work closely with teachers and staff to understand their responsibilities, their goals, and their roles in making the schools work for students. Use these understandings to support improved performance. If the primary purpose is to meet a legal requirement and the prescribed approach is restrictive, recognize evaluation as an important ritual that must be carefully observed. Find other avenues for relevant staff development and growth. In either case, the principal is accountable for faculty and staff performance.

REFLECTING ON WORKING WITH, SUPPORTING, AND SUPERVISING STAFF

Ask yourself the following questions. Then reflect on why you answered the way you did and what skills you need to hone to improve your ability to work with, support, and supervise staff.

How often do I

- use staff meetings as opportunities for trust building or staff development?
- thank a staff member?
- try to motivate individual faculty members?
- informally observe classes?
- talk informally with teachers about teaching and learning?
- work on teaching skills with teachers?
- encourage faculty to try new instructional strategies?
- model effective teaching techniques?
- communicate high expectations to faculty, staff, and students?
- help teachers develop specific strategies for improving student achievement?
- observe the librarian, school psychologist, and other professionals who work with students outside the classroom?
- spend time getting to know the jobs of noncertified staff who work inside and outside the classroom?

How comfortable am I

- telling teachers, staff, and students the truth?
- substitute teaching in one of my classrooms?
- demonstrating one or more effective instructional strategies to teachers?
- asking questions about what staff members do?
- listening to staff members' job-related problems?
- making judgments about how well teachers teach?

What do I know about

♦ staff job descriptions?

♦ cooperative learning, problem-based learning, technology, team-teaching, and other innovative instructional strategies relevant to my school?

♦ legal and contractual requirements regarding faculty and staff evaluation?

♦ various models of supervision?

♦ local, state, and national staff development resources and opportunities?

NICK FREEMAN: INVESTING IN PEOPLE AS A PRIORITY

Nick brooded about how to handle staff supervision. When he was a teacher, one of Nick's favorite sports was spotting the poor teachers and criticizing the principal for not doing something about them. Everything looked different now. Even dealing with the performance and needs of support staff overwhelmed him. The district office was calling for updates of support staff job descriptions.

At the beginning of the year, Nick felt he had so little understanding of what each staff member did that he wasn't qualified to deal with it. As the year progressed, however, he developed strong opinions about nearly everyone's position. In some cases, he needed to restrict work more and insist that people focus on the main purpose of their roles. In other cases, he needed staff to see their roles as more than a single task. The receptionist needed to see herself as an ambassador with both visitors and faculty. The secretary Nick inherited, and who was not about to voluntarily transfer to another building, needed to do her own filing and typing rather than delegating it to others and then closing her door to clip coupons. Nick did not deal with this the first semester, in part because he was amazed that anyone would operate that way.

At the same time, Nick was frustrated with his ability to influence what he knew best: teaching and learning. At the beginning of the first year he dropped in on classes frequently if irregularly. Because he wanted to make informal visits before engaging in evaluation, he was late getting the evaluation cycle started. Eight new teachers who needed to be evaluated three times before March made the chore more imposing. When the March 1 deadline for completing all evaluations and making recommendations for retention and remediation came around, Nick had met with all the nontenured faculty, but still needed to go through a preobservation conference, observation, and postobservation conference with five tenured teachers. Three other tenured teachers had not yet been in for their postobservation conferences.

At the end of his first year, Nick had met the "letter of the law," but he knew he had had little impact on the way anyone in the building went about their business. He never did get around to updating job descriptions for support staff. He certainly did not change the way even one teacher approached instruction.

Nick didn't know which would be more difficult, supervising noncertified staff, including his secretary, or effectively supervising faculty. Both tasks required more time than Nick had to give. He decided to start working with support staff during June and August when everyone was under contract (only a skeleton crew worked during July).

He began by calling a meeting of support staff. The group included secretaries from the school's main office, the assistant principal's office, and the counseling center. Also present were classroom aides, the head (full-time) cook, and the librarian's assistants (technology and media). Nick used a short warmup to make people a bit more comfortable. Then he announced that he had sensed during the past year some dissatisfaction with the working conditions for noncertified staff. He asked them to use index cards to list concerns, one per card. Nick carefully read each card and listed the items on a large newsprint sheet taped to the wall. Then he asked the group which they would like to begin discussing.

After an uncomfortable silence, one of the secretaries said she wanted to talk about how teachers treated anyone who wasn't a teacher, especially secretaries. She was tired of being looked down on, and she resented that teachers thought whatever she did was so unimportant they could interrupt her with their work at any time. The media assistant concurred and explained that teachers thought nothing of interrupting him in the middle of inventory or repairs to have him get them something they just now thought they might need. Others began to speak up on the same topic. They agreed that teachers seemed to think that they could not possibly be working on something important and so were just passing time until teachers came along to give them "real work," like making copies or fetching supplies.

A tense silence followed the group critique of teachers. After a few minutes, during which Nick resisted the temptation to try to get the ball rolling again, the technology assistant from the library remarked, "I would like to say something about how we all get along with each other. I'm the one who wrote 'staff cooperation.' It seems to me that we never help each other out. I know that Julie stays late at least once a month to get a mailing out and that no one stays to help her. I think we could all do our jobs better if we would help each other. What are we afraid of, having to do a little more work? Do you all think someone is going to take advantage of you? I don't know about you, but it seems to me that if one of us goofs up and doesn't get something done, we'll all look bad." The secretary from the counseling center added, "Well, you remember what the last principal and his assistant told us. At evaluation time we each had to stand on our own, and we weren't doing anyone or the school any favors by covering for others who couldn't do their jobs. They made it real clear we were to stick to our jobs and keep our noses out of everyone's business. That's fine with me. I don't want to make someone else look good, only to let something go I'm supposed to be doing and get a poor evaluation."

Nick worked with the support staff to set priorities for the next year. Professionalizing their work so that they saw themselves as an integral part of the educational goals of the school became their theme for the year. They also thought that this would help them work better with teachers. Nick promised the support staff that they could have regular meetings at the same times that academic departments met so that they could continue to sort out what operating as a professional group meant to them. (He made a mental note to figure out how to cover the telephones during that time—parent volunteers, maybe?) Nick agreed to continue to help them find ways in which they could collaborate to get big jobs done without threatening job descriptions and evaluations.

Nick's desire to find a better way to assist faculty yet meet requirements for formal evaluations seemed to him a nearly insurmountable task. He decided to approach this a little at a time. His first step was to meet with the faculty advisory council, which was a holdover from the former principal. Unfortunately, under the prior leadership the faculty advisory council had become mostly a forum for complaints. The council had tried to be more helpful during Nick's "honeymoon" year, but by the end of the year the temptation to revert to former behaviors had become evident. He had to figure out a way to use this council to create a better relationship between support staff and teachers. He also had to figure out a way to involve this group in finding ways that supervision and staff development could support Whitney's mission and beliefs.

Just before school started in August, Nick called the faculty advisory council together. He thanked members for their support of the past year as he struggled to learn to be a good principal. "Now," he explained to the council, "our real work begins. We need to begin to live Whitney's mission statement, 'Learning together for life.'" Nick explained that the next steps must consider the need to establish a climate of respect and trust among the adults in the building. He also explained that as principal he needed a staffing plan that recognized individual strengths and contributions to the mission. He also shared his concerns regarding the needs of support staff to feel that they were a part of the effort. By the end of that meeting, the faculty advisory committee agreed, with some reservations, to become the faculty and staff advisory committee. They also agreed to work with Nick and the certified and noncertified members of Whitney's "professional" staff to plan and submit to the district office a series of staff development possibilities available to all the adults who worked in the school.

Nick gambled a bit with his substitute teacher budget, spending some money early so that the six faculty members on the faculty and staff advisory council could miss an entire day of classes. The council used the day to examine the mission, beliefs, and data about professional development needs gathered the year before and to put together some recommendations for staff development. Their recommendations included scheduling technology workshops and tutoring sessions in their building on district staff development days. That way staff members could learn to use the hardware and software that had been installed more than a year before. They also recommended that faculty/staff meetings be used primarily as miniworkshops on teaching, with each department, including counseling, having responsibility for a workshop.

Nick convinced the council that they needed to take some responsibility for leading staff development. The council members agreed to meet with a central office staff development specialist to learn how to introduce each faculty meeting with short team-building activities. They also decided to present decision-making workshops at three of the faculty meetings. Three members agreed to serve as mentors to the new faculty members. They reviewed the school year calendar to identify various deadlines and special events. Based on the calendar, they divided responsibilities for acquainting the new faculty members with responsibilities associated with the deadlines and special events as the year progressed. The support staff representative offered to work with her "department" to put together a comprehensive package of deadlines and forms used by teachers and office personnel and to acquaint the new teachers with how and when to use each item.

The council was reluctant to make any recommendations early in the year regarding job descriptions and supervision. It seemed to everyone that this was an administrative responsibility beyond their capacity to address. They did agree to serve as a sounding board for Nick regarding his approach to supervision throughout the year. Nick was willing to settle for this for now. At least the door was open. Maybe, if the staff development plan was accepted by the district office and went well this year, he would be able to generate more interest in collaboratively tackling real issues related to supervision and evaluation. In the meantime, he vowed to change the tone of each conference by reviewing Whitney's mission and beliefs and asking teachers to help him better understand how what they did related to the beliefs and mission. He also planned to keep a tally of instructional challenges he observed. If they seemed to pile up in identifiable categories, he could provide some useful feedback to the faculty and staff advisory council regarding future staff development needs.

7

ASSESSING AND MONITORING STUDENT PROGRESS

All efforts of principals, teachers, and school staff are directed towards improving students' acquisition of knowledge and skills. The primary product of schools, learning, must be the criterion against which the utility of these efforts is evaluated. Learning is one of the more difficult things to discern.

Some have suggested that if God had delayed creation until technology had advanced, we would have emerged with a tiny electronic display in our foreheads that glows green when learning occurs. This would considerably simplify the task of teachers. Unfortunately, Eden's technological limitations apparently precluded the use of such instrumentation. Ever since, schools have instead had to rely on tests to assess what learning has taken place.

The uproar caused by *A Nation at Risk,* published in 1983 by the National Commission on Excellence in Education, and *A Nation Prepared: Teachers for the 21st Century,* published in 1986 by the Carnegie Forum, focused squarely on student achievement. Education's critics were suddenly fortified by national and international data that compared America's students with students of other nations. This was no more than a reflection of a trend on which we commented earlier: the internationalization of education. Unfortunately, the reflections weren't always that flattering: America seemed to score above Antarctica, but fared poorly in comparison with the industrialized nations of the world.

Educators found themselves poorly armed to combat data from achievement tests they could not explain. Suddenly educators' professional judgments about how students were doing were not enough. Johnny must not only be able to read. He must be able to read to world-class standards, and his school must be accountable for his achievement.

LEADERSHIP MATTERS TO STUDENT ACHIEVEMENT

Before we turn to the nitty-gritty of assessment, let us consider the fundamental question: Do principals affect student achievement? Yes! The achievement of students reflects the impact of good leadership within the school. Some schools are more challenging than others, but no school succeeds without a good principal who keeps in mind that the ultimate goal is academic success for students.

In a 1987 interview, Richard Andrews described a study that linked the work of principals to student achievement in 100 schools. Teacher judgments of their principals as instructional leaders led to the categorization of schools in this study. Strong leaders established a clear vision for their schools. They located the resources teachers needed to do their jobs well. They also had a visible presence in schools. Teachers wanted them in classrooms and took their advice about teaching. The study analyzed achievement scores over two years. Achievement of students in schools with strong leaders progressed during the study. Achievement of students in schools whose principals were not seen as strong leaders lost ground (Brandt, 1987).

Remember the "beeper" study we described in an earlier chapter? This study not only helped us understand how principals think about their work, but it also traced a link between those thoughts and the achievement of their students. For each school in the study, results on standardized, state-administered tests of reading and mathematics existed for third, sixth, and eighth grade students. The relationship between leadership and student achievement was consistently positive at all three grades. That is, as leadership scores rose, student achievement rose; as leadership scores fell, student achievement fell. The study found that the principal's role in supervising teaching and keeping the mission at the center of the school's work was strongly related to student success (Scott, Krug, & Ahadi, 1990).

Although it may seem like a long way from the principal's office to the classroom, principals make a difference to student achievement. Probably most important is the principal as visionary and promoter of the vision. The principal's role as decision-maker is to assure that decisions support rather than detract from the mission. The principal's involvement in instruction through supervision of teaching and curriculum is also related to student achievement. Creating a climate of collaboration and professional relationships contributes to the ability of teachers to plan and implement effective instruction as well.

A strong vision, a professional relationship with teachers, and a well-designed curriculum are only part of the student achievement equation. Schools cannot control some parts of the equation, such as students' home lives and wealth. Principals can use the mission to communicate and reinforce high expectations for student achievement. Keeping the mission in front of students and teachers expresses faith in the ability of students to perform academically. It stresses the importance of achieving to teachers and students. It demonstrates the value of academic success. In keeping with the mission and high expectations, schools can control the match between teaching and assessment. Schools can use student achievement data to improve instruction.

WHAT DO PRINCIPALS REALLY NEED TO KNOW ABOUT ASSESSMENT?

Of the five dimensions of leadership on which we focus, monitoring student progress appears to involve the most technical knowledge. Interpersonal skills are clearly central to the effectiveness with which a principal is able to communicate the school's educational mission, work with teachers to solve curriculum issues, and support their instructional strategies. Somehow those skills seem easier to acquire and strengthen than others that allow someone to review test results critically and act on them intelligently. Most people feel about as comfortable with test results as they do standing on a bed of quicksand. Just when they feel they might be getting somewhere, something shifts. Different numbers seem to lead in different directions. As a consequence, many ignore test results vigorously. Perhaps the logic runs something like this: "I'm an intelligent person and I can't make sense out of this, so it must be wrong or irrelevant."

Principals need to feel comfortable with a role in which they evaluate student performance because they are often the only ones in the school able to take an integrative view. Teachers tend to focus primarily on their classroom and the students they currently serve. It is more difficult for them to position the learning patterns of their students within the broader fabric of what is going on across the school. This is the pivotal role the principal can play.

The reluctance of educational professionals to come to grips with assessment issues probably stems from their pre-service preparation: they have little or no training in this area. What training exists often seems to focus on statistical issues that have less relevance to the everyday world of assessment than to topics that fit nicely in a text book. How many people memorized the definitions of and differences among nominal, ordinal, interval, and ratio scales? How many learned the variety of reliability calculations without exactly understanding the practical impact reliability has on decisions that people make? A few stalwarts probably even learned that a test's validity may not exceed the square root of its reliability. That isn't a terribly useful piece of knowledge for people who are struggling to figure out whether there's any point in using a test score after standard errors of measurement and prediction have been factored in. After all, if error is such a prominent feature of test scores, maybe we shouldn't be using them to inform important decisions.

Without the little green forehead indicator, principals must come to grips with a variety of test results. Teachers construct and administer tests, many on a regular basis. Districts typically require some form of standardized assessment across schools. Most states have established testing programs in response to the cry for accountability that accompanied publication of *A Nation at Risk*. Although some critics have suggested that students spend more time in testing than in instruction, the time devoted to testing in most curricula is relatively small. Nevertheless, the results of time spent in testing can have great value in advancing the school's educational mission, aligning curriculum in meaningful ways, and shaping and supporting the instructional practices of teachers.

Still, when the latest set of test results arrive on the principal's desk, the first reaction is quite often one of panic. The pile is high, and incomprehensible numbers fill each page. How is the principal to resist the tendency to move the pile to the closest file cabinet? How can the principal use the information to the school's advantage? How can the principal become an informed critic and user of the information test results provide?

The answer is to keep a few basic principles in mind. None of them need necessarily involve tremendous statistical sophistication. Alternatively, they do involve a good dose of common sense. Essentially, the technical features of tests reduce to three critical criteria about which the user needs to be knowledgeable, particularly about the "why" of these criteria. Why are they important? What practical impact do they have on judgments people make with test scores? These three criteria are validity, reliability, and fairness.

VALIDITY

The most fundamental property of a test score is that it leads to accurate inferences. This is the test's validity. All other properties are subordinate to validity. If the test score has no meaning, it is useless. The score may be reliable and it may be fair. That is something like saying a car has a great transmission and a superb ride but lacks a motor. You won't get anywhere with it.

So it is with tests. Students have experienced a testing explosion since questioning the quality of schools became a national pastime in the mid-1980s. Improving schools has become synonymous with increased testing and new forms of testing. Virtually every state tests students in mathematics and language arts. Many also test students in science and social studies. Most commonly, states test students for purposes of accountability, instructional improvement, and program evaluation. Most state tests use multiple choice formats, and nearly half use extended-response, open-ended items (Ryan, 1995). These state tests are, of course, in addition to tests already in use by classroom teachers and districts.

What is significant about all this testing is its varied purposes. State level testing doesn't always measure the extent to which students master locally controlled curriculum. Curriculum and instruction are often decided locally, despite national and state incursions. Local schools must make determinations regarding student achievement of the curriculum.

Consequently, the first question that must be asked when considering the results of a test is, "To what extent are the test objectives aligned with the curriculum?" If a test is not well aligned, it is likely to be insensitive to even the most ardent instructional practices. On the other hand, there is a tendency to dismiss test results, particularly those that evolve from programs outside the individual classroom, as being irrelevant to what is taught. The other side of the coin is to ask whether what is being taught is the intended curriculum. One advantage of standardized achievement tests lies in their ability to place many different programs and practices on a level playing field. The results of teacher-made tests are sometimes at odds with those from other arenas because they reflect a unique curricular perspective. A teacher may validly pursue a curriculum designed to enhance student self-esteem and develop assessments that encourage and motivate students. Of course, the students must still be able to read, count, and write to compete in today's marketplace, no matter how high their self-esteem.

Any form of student assessment, whether teacher developed, textbook, testing company, performance, or portfolio, must have meaning for students and teachers. Students find meaning in assessment when they believe that assessment relates directly to what they studied. Students deserve an answer to the question, "Will this be on the test?" Principals should expect the answer to be, "Yes, but maybe not the way you expect. You will be held responsible for the material and the skills." Problems of what will be on the test usually decrease when assessment occurs regularly and takes multiple forms.

Students also find meaning in the consequences of assessment. To what extent do assessment results affect their future? Can students use results to improve their work? Will assessment result in redoing a unit or piece of work? Will assessment mean going on to a new subject or skill? Will results be reported home, to the next teacher, to the university, or to others? Will results affect promotion or graduation? Students need to understand the purposes of assessments, the processes of those assessments, and their consequences.

Principals need to ask questions about the many assessments teachers and students encounter. What evidence makes the principal, faculty, and public confident that the tests measure students' mastery of the school's curriculum? In this age of test design, makers of achievement tests are capable of working with a clearly written curriculum, with clear expectations for students, to customize achievement tests to meet local purposes. Off-the-shelf tests about which no dialogue between the school and testing company has occurred should be suspect.

Assessment questions should also go through the classroom door. Principal and teacher discussions about students and instruction should include assessment. The issue of test validity provides a useful frame for these kinds of discussions. What are teachers doing to link student evaluation to the curriculum? What evidence can teachers provide that what is tested is what they teach? Do teachers use a variety of assessment processes? Are the assessment processes appropriate for the material and the students? Do students practice being tested? Do classroom assessment practices parallel the testing format? Or do students see the assessment format for the first time during high-stakes testing? For example, chemistry students may test their understanding of the properties of several chemicals through a paper-and-pencil test, computer simulation, or laboratory experiment. English students may test their understanding of *Romeo and Juliet* by paper-and-pencil tests, acting and interpretation of scenes from the play, panel discussions, written character analysis, or group projects about the play and Elizabethan England. Cumulative examinations may be traditional seat exams or demonstrations of learning acquired during the semester.

RELIABILITY

Once a test's validity has been confirmed for the intended purpose, it is necessary to consider its reliability. Although it is presented many different ways in textbooks, reliability assesses the extent to which the test score has meaning over some change in condition. To what extent would a similar test rank examinees in the same order?

From an achievement perspective, perhaps the most important change of condition we are usually interested in evaluating is the extent to which a different set of test items would rank students equivalently. Would a different set of mathematics problems lead to the same conclusions about who is doing well in math? If students answered questions about a different reading passage, would they seem to read as well? Questions on the test about the American war of independence inquire primarily about colonial-British battles. Are students as aware of economic factors that precipitated the war as they are about its military details?

The reason a test score must be reliable should be obvious. If you can't generalize from a test score to students' perform-ance on many other types of questions, the test score is of little help in understanding what they really know. In the extreme, if a test was to have no reliability, it would mean that we could say nothing beyond one particular set of items about what stu-dents know.

One practical consequence of considering a test score's reli-ability follows from a consideration of the test's length. As the number of items we ask students decreases, the degree of con-fidence we can have in our ability to generalize to other situa-tions decreases. What this means is that, as we reduce testing time, our ability to construct believable pictures of the progress students are making is seriously affected.

The reason that more testing occurs in classrooms today probably stems from the fact that too little occurred in the past. Much of what occurred was of questionable validity. The mar-ket in student achievement didn't suddenly plummet in 1983 just before *A Nation at Risk* appeared. Instead, the erosion was gradual and took place over many decades. The lack of system-atic assessment systems that produced valid and reliable data for comparing schools and districts probably contributed to that erosion. How many people would feel comfortable living near a nuclear power reactor whose operation was checked only on a monthly or even weekly basis? If we believe the con-sequences of schooling are important, then we need to affirm that belief by conducting regular, systematic checks of those consequences that produce valid and reliable data.

FAIRNESS

The concern about fairness in testing might, at first glance, appear to be correlated with America's increasing multicultural-ism. While multiculturalism certainly energized concern about fairness, the notion is more fundamental. Test scores must have the same meaning for different groups of people, whether those groups break along ethnic-racial lines, gender lines, or other-wise. Quite simply, if the test is supposed to assess math proficiency, the score should have the same meaning for boys and girls. More generally, the test should not disadvantage any group of students.

How can a test do so? Informally, it happens when a test makes different demands on different groups of students. For example, the test might appear to be a math test. But the vocabulary of word problems in the test may exceed that required to assess a student's math proficiency. For some students, those with lower vocabulary skills, the test may not be a challenge to their math skills but to their ability to understand complicated vocabulary.

EVALUATING VALIDITY, RELIABILITY, AND FAIRNESS

It should be clear by now that validity, reliability, and fairness can only be evaluated reasonably when the reviewer has a good understanding of the test's objectives and its content. There is a tendency sometimes to dismiss these concerns too flippantly, by recourse to statistical indexes. For example, the test reports a reliability coefficient of .95. It must be good. A seasoned teacher developed the items; they must be valid. The test manual has extensive tables related to the test's fairness that look impressive. This must not be a problem.

The reality is that many tests constructed by experienced teachers have relatively little validity because item writers work without a clear purpose for the test. Similarly, a reliability coefficient of .95 could mean the test focuses on a very limited set of objectives. It produces scores that generalize only over a very narrow range of content.

Do principals need to be statistical experts to advance the educational mission of the school? No. They need to be comfortable with judgments they make about a test's validity, reliability, or fairness if they are to merge results from different instruments and different sources into a single mosaic. Because of the technical aspects of testing—and no one is suggesting that these aspects are insignificant—there is a tendency to mistrust judgment, to substitute secondhand claims for firsthand review, or to dismiss results as irrelevant or unusable.

The point we advance here is that the leadership role of the principal requires a degree of comfort with test results. Whether they are used for good or bad largely rests on the principal's initiative.

USE DATA TO IMPROVE STUDENT PERFORMANCE

Teachers find meaning in assessment that helps them better assist individual students and their class as a whole. Certainly teachers use assessment as a sorting mechanism. Which students are the bluebirds? Which students are college-bound? Which students will we retain this year? Assessments should serve a more immediate and practical purpose, helping teachers help students. Noting that a student or group of students does poorly and continuing to document poor achievement does nothing to assist the students. Principals and teachers need to work together to use assessment data to adjust classroom organization, daily routines, teaching materials, and instructional strategies so that what happens to students is dependent on their demonstrated needs. The absence of data allows what happens to students to depend on something else, such as habit or comfortable practice.

Testing and other forms of assessment have many purposes. These include making informed changes in curriculum, improving classroom instruction, assisting individual students, communicating with parents and community about what happens in schools, and demonstrating accountability for tax dollars. Principals can use the data from student assessment, whether it comes from state-administered exams, purchased achievement tests, locally developed achievement tests, or teacher-developed assessments in various forms, to improve student performance.

Too many teachers and principals shut down when they hear the words "data" and "research." As we suggested earlier, their fear may arise from a limited understanding of research design, anxiety about working with numbers, and bad memories associated with graduate statistics courses. Increasing reliance on site-based management for school improvement and accountability holds principals accountable for those decisions. Principals and the other adults in the building must learn to go beyond professional instinct and point to data as one means of supporting their decisions.

The use of data for decision making can change the structures and cultures of schools so that they are more supportive of learning. Seymour Sarason (1990) warns educators that their motivation, creativity, and intellectual growth can be undercut by the structures and cultures of their schools. Roland Barth (1990) recommends that educators help students achieve success by promoting profound learning for the adults in the school. An excellent place to start profound learning for school improvement is in the use of data for making decisions.

To create learning organizations focused on the needs of students, schools need to use data to identify, define, and solve problems. Principals must educate themselves about the basics of research design and use of assessment data to inform key organizational and curricular decisions. They need to learn how to use common data-management software and should see that others know how to use it. Principals should also learn to read research articles and statistical reports critically so that they can make informed judgments regarding the conclusions being drawn by others.

Principals need to share data with teachers and other staff. One place to start is individual and collective discussions of the results of achievement tests or college entrance tests. Another is to engage in a discussion of student grades or the "D/F" lists. Discussion could occur about the results of a locally developed or adapted test designed to benchmark student progress through the schools. The point of any one of these conversations is to examine achievement data, asking questions such as: What are students really learning? Do we test what we teach? Do we teach the intended curriculum? What teaching strategies seem most effective? Are some students less well served by our curriculum and instruction than others? Is our curriculum well aligned, or are we creating gaps and unproductive overlaps in students' learning experiences?

Student achievement data can describe and evaluate more than the success of individuals or groups of students. Those data also provide principals with evidence of progress or lack of progress toward achieving the school mission and related school goals. For example, if one school goal is to serve all students, achievement data can be sorted in a variety of ways to determine the extent to which the school is successful in meeting that goal. It may be necessary to look through various lenses, such as special education, socioeconomic status, grade level, ethnicity, age, or attendance. If a school goal is to graduate 90% of the students, achievement data can give early indication of the likelihood that current strategies will be successful in achieving that goal. A school that intends to provide students with a variety of experiences from which they can learn skills not taught at home can use data from assessments to measure their success. Many, if not all, school goals can and should be measured using achievement data as indicators of progress.

Data regarding student achievement should be used as a means of communicating progress of the students and of the school toward goals to the school's stakeholders. Parents are typically interested in receiving progress reports and report cards about their children. Parents and others in the community also appreciate receiving periodic newsletters that include references to the school mission and goals and evidence that they are being achieved. A good working relationship with the local press provides opportunities, regardless of the subject of a particular news story, to explain progress. Teachers and students, too, are audiences for data about student achievement. Awards assemblies, memos, and staff meetings are excellent opportunities to share educational data. To share data effectively and appropriately, principals must learn how to analyze and interpret data. They must then be able to explain it in ways that erase the mystery from data and accurately paint a portrait of the school and its students.

Teacher evaluation conferences are suitable forums for discussing achievement data. Teachers and principals should discuss the methods teachers use to assess students in the classroom and the types of records teachers maintain. They should compare teacher assessment data of individuals and groups with other measures, such as districtwide assessments or state-administered tests. Discussions may also compare past achievement of students with current progress. Engaging in these conversations as part of the pre- or postobservation process reminds teachers that student assessment data has relevance beyond reporting to students and parents.

Part of the principal's work is to model creative thinking. The need for creative thinking becomes especially important when trying to get out of the familiar box regarding student assessment. Principals need to find ways to work with teachers to discover new and creative means of addressing curricular, instructional, and learning problems. Many of these problems become apparent when assessment data are systematically analyzed. Many of the solutions are less apparent. Solutions may involve not only changes in instruction, but changes in organization of the school. For example, to accommodate an experiential approach to language arts and social studies, long blocks of time may need to be worked into a schedule normally marked by 47-minute periods. Providing time for writing across the curriculum may mean changes in classroom instruction and team teaching by English teachers with teachers of other subjects.

REFLECTING ON ASSESSING STUDENT PROGRESS

Ask yourself the following questions. Then reflect on why you answered the way you did and what additional skills you may need to monitor student progress within the building effectively.

How often do I

- ◆ review a student's performance with a teacher?
- ◆ discuss the results of school- and districtwide tests with faculty or parents?
- ◆ review the content of teacher assessments to see how they align with the intended curriculum?
- ◆ examine the content of standardized achievement tests to determine how closely the test objectives fit with teacher instruction?
- ◆ attempt to organize test results in ways that help teachers discern and respond to trends that emerge over time?
- ◆ feel comfortable sharing test results with others inside and outside the school?

ELIZABETH HARRIS DISCOVERS WAYS IN WHICH TEST RESULTS ADVANCE CENTRAL'S MISSION

Central High School's pride rested in large part on its long history of high-achieving students. Only a small percentage of each graduating class did not go on to college. When Elizabeth met with Central's two long-time counselors in the spring of her first year to discuss student progress, she was struck by their self-congratulatory approach to the meeting. It was clear that Central's counselors saw their primary role as serving as a screening and sorting mechanism. They advised students whether to take the ACT, SAT, or no precollegiate exam. They advised students and parents on "suitable" higher education placements for their students. They believed that their goal was to produce a large number of graduates each year with higher education plans. Although the majority of students in each graduating class entered college the following autumn, Elizabeth noticed that the institutions to which students aspired had gradually changed in character over the past five years. More and more students reported attending the local community college each year.

Central's approach to reporting student achievement to the public through ACT and SAT scores disturbed Elizabeth. If counselors regularly discouraged students they labeled as community college material from taking these exams, then just how useful could the data be in either representing Central to the public or in influencing its curriculum?

During the same five-year period, Elizabeth noticed that Central had strategically been adding Advanced Placement (AP) courses. Suddenly Elizabeth found herself worried. Was Central serving well only the students destined for professions requiring large investments in higher education? Was Central perhaps unconsciously ignoring a growing part of its changing population, students whose career ambitions required different types of preparation after high school? How was she to know for sure if data about all the students were not being systematically collected and studied?

In late September of her second year, Elizabeth discussed these concerns with the superintendent. The student assistance team at Central, headed in name by a counselor but convened regularly by a teaching assistant, had a long list of students earning D's and F's. The team then worked with teachers to find individual assistance for chronically failing students. Assistance took various forms, including student tutors and study groups and direct teacher instruction outside the classroom on a regularly scheduled basis. When curricular or instructional recommendations were being made, they seemed historically to address the most successful portion of the student population and to ignore the needs of those who were least successful.

The superintendent agreed with Elizabeth that her concerns were significant. The superintendent also told her that she was wrong when she said that no data were available to judge the overall achievement of the general Central population. She remembered that each year the state education agency administered assessments at various grade levels. All Central 10th graders took tests in reading, writing, and mathematics each year. Elizabeth acknowledged that she vaguely remembered some testing days last spring. Frankly, the counselors had handled the scheduling and Elizabeth had not worried about it.

"Where are the reports on those tests?" she asked. The reports were literally sitting on the superintendent's desk, recently received from the state office. Elizabeth remembered an administrator meeting about a year earlier where the superintendent distributed each school's report and briefly discussed them in a very general way. Elizabeth was fairly sure she knew which file drawer hid last year's report. She sighed and told the superintendent that she would have to study the reports and find a way to make them meaningful. She also wondered if Central was gathering and using data not based on national and statewide tests that might be more useful in planning curriculum and instruction.

The faculty and staff advisory team was already busy with staff development, and she wanted its members to work with her on problems associated with supervision and evaluation. How could she start another large initiative without burning out her people? She just could not wait to figure out how to know more about student achievement and how to better assist students through classroom instruction. Elizabeth initially turned to the Curriculum Committee, an elected group whose primary purpose seemed to be to react to new course proposals brought forward by the departments. The Curriculum Committee had once studied and rejected the idea of block scheduling. They had also headed up preparation three years ago for the regional accreditation visit.

Elizabeth presented the Curriculum Committee with her concerns and shared information about SAT and ACT scores. She spent a great deal of time sharing comments about Central's performance on the state assessments of reading, writing, and mathematics. On average, reading scores were well above the state mean, math scores were slightly above state average, but writing scores fell below the state average by a disappointing margin. What did that mean? Elizabeth and the Curriculum Committee spent several subsequent meetings learning more about the state assessment, how items were developed and selected, and how school scores were determined. What did the state assessments measure anyway?

The state assessments, as it turned out, measured student achievement against a set of standards adopted nearly four years before by the state education agency. Central, like many other high schools, had essentially ignored the state's work or at least not considered the state standards when evaluating changes in its curriculum. Instead, Central had continued its traditional approach to curriculum, developing the high end. Even so, learning that Central 10th graders, both high and not so high achievers, fell below the state average in writing was a great disappointment.

The Curriculum Committee analyzed the writing standards and scoring rubrics used to judge student writing on the state examination. The chair of the English Department was invited to a meeting and asked to explain why Central students' writing failed to stand up when graded according to the state's criteria. The chair's natural defensiveness caused the meeting to go nowhere. Defensive postures ranged from the assertion that the students come to Central inadequately prepared (although, for this year at least, the district's 6th graders scored a bit above the state average in writing) to charges that teachers of other subjects not only ignored the quality of student writing but set bad examples themselves. Curriculum Committee members fired back that the English Department's arrogance and English teachers' preferences for teaching literature had caused them to reap what they sowed.

Elizabeth admitted to herself that it was stupid to allow the Curriculum Committee to invite the English Department chair to its meeting with no preparation or briefing. She had certainly underestimated the volatility of the subject and overestimated the Curriculum Committee's ability to behave professionally during the discussion. A few days later she met privately with the English Department chair to examine the writing report in detail. The chair agreed to discuss the report with other English faculty and to compare the goals and strategies of the state assessment with the writing processes and content taught and graded at Central.

In early November the English Department chair sought out Elizabeth to talk about writing at Central. The English faculty were sincerely concerned that all Central students were not getting ample opportunities to write in ways that would prepare them for continuing education or for employment, which was one of Central's beliefs. In part, the fault lay in the English classrooms. Many students were simply being tested on something that they had not been taught. On the other hand, the writing assessment seemed to be sufficiently complex that even good writers might not do well unless the processes being tested were part of the daily expectations all students faced when doing formal writing.

The English Department wanted to address the Curriculum Committee in a spirit of collaboration to find ways to change how Central's entire faculty and staff addressed the need for students to write well according to state standards. Elizabeth reminded the chair that this would be a major task. Getting teachers of all subjects to join the effort to improve writing would be one huge undertaking, but it would not be sufficient. Central must also find a way to collect data frequently about student writing and be prepared to use those data to change course as necessary. The challenge for the English Department, the Curriculum Committee, and Elizabeth would be to see the process through and to so imbed it in Central's daily operations that it would not appear as a short-term project forced on everyone by the English Department's "problem" with writing.

Even as the Curriculum Committee and English Department tackled this challenge, Elizabeth refrained from sharing what she knew to be a larger truth: that this process needed to be repeated for many other areas of learning. A series of small victories, she told herself, will eventually add up. This is only my second year here. Finally, I am working with curriculum!

PART III

CREATIVE AND CRITICAL THINKING

8

PROBLEM SOLVING

Solving problems has less to do with knowing answers than with being able to think well. As principal, you want to be able to process information, appreciate other people's points of view, and make sense out of ill-structured situations that have ramifications beyond the initial problem.

Principals who are effective at what they do never quit reading and learning. They understand that school challenges are messy, because every problem is a people problem. Even decisions made on pieces of paper affect real people's lives. Effective principals understand that the core elements of most problems have been explored by others in other settings. Familiarity with current educational literature contributes to the art of making sense of ill-structured situations. They also understand how to use research to gather data that lead to sound decisions. They help teachers engage in action research that informs immediate classroom situations and enables planning for future situations and students. If you intend to lead your building through present challenges into a brighter future, you must believe that the status quo is never new enough. You must model lifelong learning as a standard operating procedure for other educators. Visibly being a learner, even after receiving advanced degrees, models lifelong learning for others. Continuing to be a learner is a necessity for effective principals. Only principals who are blind to changes in the world and blissful in their ignorance of external forces affecting their schools would shun new information. Principals who disdain their learning should not be leading the learning of others. Anyone who knows it all clearly does not know enough.

CURRENT EVENTS ARE NOT FOR SOCIAL STUDIES TEACHERS ONLY

Principals are aware that news from other nations, other states, and even the town down the road may soon affect their schools. They work to stay in touch with current events. Doing so means investing time and money. Sometimes this means spending their money on journals, books, tapes, workshops, courses, and on-line services to help them stay informed of trends, innovations, and challenges facing education. Effective principals keep in touch with current events through daily reading of local newspapers; participation in local networks; membership in regional, state, and national professional organizations; subscriptions to national education news publications; and use of on-line technology.

One useful technique is to read the local newspaper before going to school each day. Local newspapers (or in some cases, local radio programs) frequently carry stories that will affect the mood of the school. Every part of the paper has potential for school-related news. Headlines may announce merger rumors. The sports page may speculate about the eligibility of a student athlete. The education section may compare national and local SAT scores. The police blotter or court section may associate students or their relatives with crimes. A news article may report an overnight accident involving a student, teacher, or someone closely associated with the school. Principals have often already heard the news. They read as much for accuracy of the stories as to learn something new. Reading the paper is a means of preparing to deal with current events effectively and to manage surprising questions or assumptions by others.

Formal local networks provide principals with opportunities to become informed about current or future events. Community service organizations that meet regularly for breakfast or lunch are one means of creating rapport with formal and informal community leaders. Regular attendance and active participation not only demonstrate an interest in the welfare of the school's community, but also provide avenues for asking questions and being alerted to undercurrents that may evolve into overt activities.

Organized meetings of local and regional educators also form an important part of the principal's networking. Such meetings may be scheduled by a regional office of education, university, state department, professional association, or core group of principals eager for collegial conversations. Regardless of their sponsorship, meetings are valuable sources of information about pending legislation, state regulations, professional development opportunities, legal decisions, job openings, and potential problems. One of the greatest values is the opportunity to safely ask peers their advice and to think with others about creative solutions to problems. Equally valuable is expansion of the circle in which one is known, because this provides potential contacts for recruiting new faculty members and for one's own career advancement.

Professional associations play a significant role in principals' networks. Statewide professional associations provide three valuable services related to current events. First, they maintain contact with legislatures by providing ready access and means of influencing state education law. Second, they host state and regional events designed to put principals in touch with each other, share information, develop skills, and prepare for job changes. Third, professional associations publish newsletters and useful guides addressing hot issues and research-based practices.

Likewise, national professional associations host annual meetings that address a full range of contemporary issues, future trends, and skill building. Membership in national associations includes subscriptions to journals dedicated to providing administrators with access to research and theory and their on-the-job applications. Some journals are available on tape for "reading" while commuting. Principals would be well-served to invest not only in associations dedicated to serving school administrators, but in associations focusing on innovations in curriculum and staff development.

Professional journals are one means of staying in touch with national and international education events. The disadvantage of journals is that they are generally published monthly or quarterly. They may also be available only through fairly expensive memberships in professional associations, or their subscription rates may seem too high for first-year and small-school principals. Yet those with the fewest resources may be in the most need of timely educational news. Educational current events are easily accessible through weekly and biweekly publications and the wonders of technology. A modest investment will bring weekly and biweekly educational newspapers to a principal's mailbox. A modem will bring nearly every professional association, hundreds of news sources, and numerous discussion groups into a principal's office or home. Principals should explore with their librarian and those in the know about the Internet how to efficiently access these weekly print and daily computerized news sources.

INTELLECTUAL SERVICE AND SELF-SERVICE

Truly great principals love to read. Parents and school boards should be wary of principal candidates who announce they cannot name a book they have read for pleasure or professional knowledge in the past few months or who are unfamiliar with widely read journals aimed at school administrators.

Peter Senge (1990) reminds us that "Human Beings (sic) are designed for learning" (p. 7). He laments the controlling forces of society's institutions that reward people for performances and right answers rather than for superior learning and creativity that will eventually lead to superior performance. Senge urges leaders to integrate thinking and acting at all levels of their organizations. Characteristics of learning organizations include vision, creative tension, adaptivity, systems thinking, and new leadership roles. The new leader must be a designer, a teacher, and a steward. To fulfill these roles simultaneously, leaders must develop skills in building a shared vision, developing and testing mental models that challenge traditional assumptions, and thinking systemically about underlying trends and change forces.

What does this have to do with reading? Everything. Principals have the capacity to redesign schools. The way in which principals use their influence affects the very culture of their schools. Choices principals make affect the social structures of schools. Principals can choose to use their influence to redesign their organizations so that the formal and informal structures better serve students. They understand that organizational design has more to do with how people work together than with job titles and job descriptions. They seek knowledge about how to improve the quality of that work through better design.

Creative designers constantly seek new materials that allow nontraditional designs. Constantly browsing the literature allows designers to be among the first to notice new materials. Keeping in touch with professionals across the country and around the globe enables designers to have advanced notice of innovations in design technology. Reading in fields other than their own makes it possible for designers to adapt ideas, materials, and technology from other fields to improve their own. One of the defining characteristics of principals of improving schools is that they find tools to improve productivity of individuals and groups.

Principals expand the capacity of their organizations to learn when they take on the role of teacher. As the head learner and head teacher, principals must help everyone in the school develop a sense of reality (Senge, 1990). Doing so requires challenging organization members' narrow personal perspectives on the organization. All have framed the organization within the narrow door of their classrooms, the views over their counters, the slice of the student body with which they work, or their cycle of duties. Expanding their image of their organization is possible for principals who are in touch with opportunities for others to learn information and skills that will enrich their lives in the organization. Understanding the entire organization from a systems perspective is critical if each adult working with the school is to operate as a member of a team from a shared vision. In the role of teacher, principals purposely seek professional development for faculty and staff as well as for themselves. They may serendipitously discover new opportunities. Neither happens unless the principal constantly reads and networks with other professionals.

Career educators see teaching and administration as a calling, not just a way to make a living. Most enter education out of a sense of a higher calling. Teaching is more than meeting students each day to feed them a prescribed curriculum. Working in schools is a means of improving society, furthering democracy, and helping young people find meaning for their lives.

Because being a principal is a means of helping other adults do this important work, the role of steward comes naturally to principals. According to Senge (1990), stewardship has to do with caring about the people in the organization and caring for the larger purpose of the organization. Stewards protect the wellness of people committed to the organization and the organization's vision. Ignorant leaders cannot effectively exercise this protective role, which includes helping people take care of themselves. Nor can leaders who withhold information and opportunities from people exercise it.

Effective stewards participate in the intellectual and practical world beyond their organizations and encourage others to do the same. Effective principals realize that service to their organizations includes taking leadership roles in professional and service organizations. Every role requires reading and networking to acquire new knowledge. By continuing to learn through these connections, they encourage others to participate in learning and leadership activities outside the school. Teachers who take leadership roles in associations, staff development organizations, government grants, university task forces, book discussion groups, and similar activities enrich themselves and bring new resources to the organization.

THE ROLE OF REFLECTION

Thinking is more than an intellectual exercise. Thinking is not something we do only in school or just to get the right answer. Thinking is more than responding to a stimulus or even to a crisis. Thinking is both a satisfying activity and a means to an end. In schools, we want to continually think about how to improve the ways in which our schools serve our children.

Self-reflection goes beyond second guessing. For example, it begins after hours when the principal and assistant principal discuss ways they reacted to a confrontation between a student and teacher. Their conversation includes much more than what happened and what could have happened. Because they trust each other, they talk about how they felt when it happened. They include discussion of their values and the conflicts the incident created for them. Their discussion may more clearly define some values. They may plan new actions for the future.

Self-reflection occurs in the car on the way to school as a principal mentally rehearses a presentation to the superintendent or a discussion with a parent. Considerations of strategy and language are part of the self-talk. Self-coaching and encouraging mingle with practiced sentences and mental lists of what to include. The result may be a calmer demeanor or more professional presentation.

Roland Barth (1990) reminds us that self-reflection is essential to building communities of learners. The flurry of rhetoric regarding the idea of learning communities would have us all believe that our schools have been somehow transformed into such places. But to be a community of learners, a school must fully commit to creating the conditions under which the principal, students, and teachers "become serious, committed, sustained, lifelong, cooperative learners" (p. 45).

To create such conditions, principals must make a conscious effort to engage in reflection that leads to profound learning about themselves. Principals must find time in their busy days or weeks for thinking about themselves. Their reflections should center on personal issues associated with personal and professional shortcomings, analysis of real and hypothetical problems, humor and other emotions, risks, and the higher purposes associated with the job of principal.

Reflective time is personal time. For some, reflection takes place while exercising. Others prefer to sit in a quiet spot. A few go further, using spiritual or meditative techniques to inspire rich reflections. Many find satisfaction in writing their thoughts. Certainly the very act of finding the words to write down important ideas causes more intense reflection than stream of consciousness thinking. An old fashioned approach to reflection is the keeping of a diary. Another is writing to a pen pal. Modern technology makes both more doable. Miniature tape recorders make dictating reflections just before sleeping, at waking, or on the move convenient. Computers on desktops, on laps, and even in-hand make writing more convenient and expedient. E-mail makes daily notes to pen pals practical.

Writing or dictating thoughts, reactions, ideas, concerns, and plans provides an emotional and creative outlet for those engaged in a demanding and isolating job. Reflective writing also provides a means of testing ideas and reactions. Returning to something written a week ago often provides a sense of perspective that could not have been present in the heat of a moment. Sharing writing with a trusted friend or colleague provides valuable opportunities for professional enrichment.

RESEARCH IS PRACTICAL

Research has power. Consideration of good data leads to making good decisions. Principals who understand the power and potential of making research and data-based decisions model, mentor, and encourage schoolwide use of research designed to provide the organization with evidence of changes and need for change.

Teachers and principals shudder at the thought of doing research. Perhaps because of too rigid understandings of what constitutes "research" they carry with them from introductory statistics courses, school professionals discount the research they do every day. Teachers constantly check on student progress by means of in-class questioning and grading of student work. This is research. Principals check on student progress by collecting weekly information on students who are failing. This is research. Assistant principals check on student progress by examining daily and weekly reports of student absences. This, too, is research. These and other data can help solve school problems.

The university understanding of research can be a helpful guide to schools interested in researching their problems of practice. It can also get in the way as design constraints and academic research agendas so alter research questions that they become meaningless to practitioners. But on the positive side, university professors, graduate assistants, and school people studying for advanced degrees can serve as valuable resources for selecting research problems, designing data gathering instruments and strategies, analyzing data, and reporting data objectively to the school and its constituents. Principals should not be shy about approaching universities to collaborate in school research partnerships. Many faculty, particularly in education and sociology departments, are eager to work with schools to address problems of practice.

Research by those inside the school organization adds to the reflective processes encouraged earlier in this chapter. School-based research systematically undertakes to study a particular aspect of the school and gathers evidence to answer questions, support assumptions, or test ideas. School-based research may vary significantly from academic research in the types of information considered as useful data. It may also differ from academic research in that the intent is not to generalize results to a larger population. Its purpose, instead, is to address a particular issue at a particular time within a particular school and community context.

Research by those inside the school to address school problems has several advantages. First, those involved in doing the research will benefit from the results. Second, school-based research usually results in the involvement of several people, creating numerous educational opportunities. Third, school-based research creates a climate supportive of learning by all members of the school community. Fourth, school-based research puts information in the hands of many, expanding power beyond a proprietary few. Fifth, school-based research enables collaborative decisions based on data as well as professional judgment.

School-based research is, in the purest sense, a means of problem solving. The process model of problem solving promoted by the National Policy Board for Educational Administration (1993) consists of several steps. Those steps may be summarized as:

- analysis of external and internal factors that affect the process and outcomes of problem analysis;
- recognition of the proble;m
- information collection, evaluation, and integration;
- reinterpretation or representation of the problem;
- identification of causal factors; and
- solution finding.

Put even more simply, every problem has two main components: a statement of the problem and the solution.

The first challenge is to be sure that we understand the real problem. When the problem initially came to our attention, we may have met a solution statement disguised as a problem. We may have seen only one aspect of a very complicated problem. We may find we are looking not at a problem at all, but at symptoms of an as yet unidentified problem. To come up with a true statement of the problem, we must answer the following questions. What is the disharmony or undesirable situation we are facing? Is it really a problem, or is it a situation that current policies or rules clearly address? What facts do we know? What emotional, social, political, or educational factors will influence our ability to collect information and implement a solution? What information is needed from or about individuals, the school organization, and outside resources? What resources (financial, time, access) will we need to study?

To use research to solve problems, the problem itself must be clear. The most difficult work of research may be in asking the right questions. Principals can use the untapped knowledge of faculty, staff, students, parents, and others to help shape the right questions. Questions can then be refined through analysis of related educational literature. Don't overlook your school librarian, local libraries, interlibrary loan systems, electronic communications processes, professional associations, state departments of education, and universities as sources that can help inform and shape your thinking. Finally, frame all questions within the context of the school's mission. Answering the question and solving the problem must promote the school mission.

The first step in problem solving is to consider what information will help answer the question. Educators collect lots of data. Most of it is quantifiable. Much of it remains in file cabinets because it is of no use in addressing real problems of practice. Helpful data, whether expressed in numbers or words, are easy to understand. No expert interpretation is required. Helpful data relate directly to the problem at hand and have meaning to those dealing with the problem. Useful data are free of subjectivity. That is, the information is not colored by the perspectives of those doing the collecting or reporting. Data have little value if hoarded. Data must be shared with those affected by the situation under study.

Problem solving also requires skill in integrating and interpreting resource information and data. In this sense, problem solving is like good teaching. The teacher's ability to synthesize complex concepts and present them clearly to students is the same ability necessary for the synthesis and presentation of data collected about the school. Integration of resources and data may lead to redefining the problem and a clearer understanding of influences on the problem's birth and solution. Several solutions will probably present themselves. Alone or in collaboration with others, principals must select a solution appropriate for their school.

Problem solving requires both keeping a professional distance from the emotional interests of other individuals and constantly checking on the influence of our values. Remember that great principals are clear about their values. They make decisions, including that very important decision about which school(s) they are willing to lead, based in large part on their comfortable relationships with their values. Principals' visions of schools and their school missions are intimately connected with their values. During the problem-solving process, principals constantly check that the mission of the school and their values are not violated. A violation of either is cause for re-thinking the solution or for resignation.

What kinds of problems might be addressed, in part, by us-ing and doing research in schools? The first that comes to mind are problems of the classroom. For example, what classroom management processes result in increased time on task for stu-dents? What is the most effective means of teaching critical thinking skills to elementary students? How might a group of students known to be difficult to handle be motivated to posi-tively contribute to the classroom? What kind of relationship between regular and special education teachers is most effec-tive when special education students are part of the general education classroom?

Questions of school organization that affect the classroom also come to mind. Do students acquire greater subject area and critical thinking skills in traditional 47-minute classes, or do they perform better in scheduled blocks of time? What im-pact does the inclusion of a study skills curriculum have on student performance? What impact does an advisor-advisee program have on student attitudes toward school? Does a par-ent education program result in students being more ready to learn when they begin kindergarten?

Certainly, questions concerning school climate deserve re-search. For example, a principal may find that working col-laboratively with teachers is very difficult. Small groups and individuals continually lobby for special consideration even after a collective decision has been made through a series of faculty or committee meetings. Introducing noncertified staff to the efforts to collaborate continually results in work groups that disintegrate. The principal has a sense for the problem, but probably needs to gather two kinds of data, some that will help to better define the problem and some that will help solve the problem. At the bottom line, the principal can begin develop-ing collaborative relationships by involving faculty and staff in defining the problem, gathering relevant data, and using the data to guide solutions. Jumping into a major staff develop-ment project on team building would be premature.

None of these questions is easily answered. A rich litera-ture base presents theories and data supporting different ap-proaches and perspectives on each of these and other questions about schools. The literature base can help sharpen your questions and support research designs so that your school can make decisions best for its students.

PROBLEM SOLVING IS A GROUP ACTIVITY

Principals cannot solve the problems of schools alone. Neither can consultants or professional researchers. Understanding of problems shared by schools across the nation and internationally helps us think about the problems we face locally. Just as the final decisions about curriculum are local, even in the face of world-class standards, so decisions about which problems are important and how they are to be addressed are also local. Principals who solve larger problems of local organization and practice alone may find themselves the only ones implementing the solutions.

No school is problem-free. For example, our heroine Elizabeth took on a prize principalship in a school of high-achieving students supported by ambitious parents—at least, that's the way Central presented itself to her. Even this high-achieving environment presents some very real problems associated with curriculum, student achievement, collegiality, and professional development. Elizabeth initially identified some problem areas, but chose not to own these problems herself. In doing so, Elizabeth modeled her value that the most important relationship in the school was between teachers and students. She did so by involving teachers and support staff in decisions about professionalism and curriculum. If she is to continue to model problem solving, however, Elizabeth must never be satisfied. Even as she pushed Central's Curriculum Committee to challenge traditional models of teaching writing, she knew that she would have to challenge her school's historical practices in other areas eventually. She could continue to prick the consciousness of others through her words. Eventually that would get old. What she needed, instead, was to create an environment in which challenging what is common becomes common itself.

How does a school institutionalize the questioning of practice? How do those who work in the school come to identify and solve important problems? Just as the principal must continue to learn, so must others in the school, if the school is to face and solve its problems. The principal can formally and informally support professional learning as part of a larger professional development plan in several ways. For example, share what you read with others, in conversation, in written summaries, and in quotations added to staff announcements and parent/community newsletters. Start discussion groups of teachers, staff, parents, and community members to read and study the works of current authors writing in educational and organizational areas of interest to your school. Co-teach or guest speak in college and university classrooms. Lead a professional development activity for teachers or other administrators at the district, regional, state, or national level. Engage a local group of teachers, administrators, or others in study of a phenomenon that may affect your area soon. Go back to school for an advanced degree and discuss what you read and learn with your superintendent, assistant principal, department chairs, secretary, and others. Join electronic bulletin board or news groups focusing on areas of concern to your school and share what you learn with others. Develop a home page for your school and use it to collect information from those who access it regarding "problems" potentially facing your school.

Only your imagination limits your ability to involve others in solving problems so that they remain solved and so that problem solving becomes a legitimate way of doing business. This type of problem solving is both preventive maintenance and expert leadership.

SELF-ASSESSMENT

Do you actively engage yourself and others in identifying and solving problems? Use these questions to reflect on your approach to identifying and solving problems.

Do you strive to learn more about potential "problems" facing schools by

- reading the local newspaper daily with an eye to items of possible concern to the school?
- reading at least one professional journal each month?
- reading three or more books each year that relate to your work as an educator?
- attending regional, state, and national meetings of groups related to your work as an educator?

- participating in local professional, governmental, or philanthropic organizations?
- reflecting on your work through writing, conversations, or other creative outlets?

Do you engage others in problem solving by

- sharing ideas from professional journals and meetings with others associated with your school?
- recommending a book or journal article to another educator or asking another for a recommendation?
- identifying problem areas to be researched and collaboratively planning a research strategy?
- involving local resource people (from colleges, universities, other organizations) in problem identification or data gathering or data interpretation?
- sharing information and data?

After you have read the above questions, take time to practice self-reflection. More likely than not, you skimmed the questions above and even mentally noted some short answers. Now, consider the questions a "problem" to be solved. That is, how can you better engage yourself and others in deciding what problems stand between your school and your vision of the school? How can you then engage your school in consciously setting out to solve these problems? How can you institutionalize the practice of questioning and solving problems so that the school continues to improve itself, even after you have left its principalship and several of the current faculty have retired? Try writing your answers to these questions. The process may be slow and painstaking. That is the nature of reflection until you practice it so often that it becomes as much a part of your being as you want problem solving to become part of the everyday work of your school.

NICK FREEMAN: BEGINNING PROBLEM SOLVING AT WHITNEY

Nick's efforts to use the faculty and staff advisory committee more effectively, beginning with creation of new staff development possibilities, provided him with a much needed feeling of progress. At the same time, with each accomplishment, Nick became increasingly aware of just how large the job of principal really is. Everything needed his attention. Some practices were easily changed habits. Other issues would require years of chipping away at values and behaviors and bureaucratic constraints. Nick decided to help himself in an effort to help his school.

During his first year as principal, Nick felt lost in the large district training meetings for principals. He kept quiet and watched and learned, but mostly he kept to himself. At subdistrict meetings, when he was part of the administrative decision making team, Nick had been careful not to say anything that would cause the superintendent or other principals to suspect he was not qualified.

He decided to become a bit more aggressive during his second year. One of the other principals at the subdistrict meeting, Jim Night, had encouraged Nick to call him if he had any questions or concerns. Although Jim was a well-respected principal, Nick had been reluctant to expose his ignorance and had not taken advantage of the offer. Before the first subdistrict principals' meeting of Nick's second year, Nick called Jim to invite him to meet for breakfast and to get better acquainted. Continuing this practice before each monthly meeting led to Jim inviting Nick to join him at a meeting sponsored by the state principals' association. At that meeting Nick met several others from both inside and outside his district who were interested in staff supervision and staff development. They encouraged Nick to explore a Web site and listserve they all used to engage in conversations about the relationship between staff development and supervision, innovations in staff development, and the links between staff development and school improvement.

Networking with other professionals led Nick to explore other resources. He joined both the principals' association and a professional staff development association. Each month he browsed the table of contents of journals he received for articles relevant to his dreams for Whitney. He occasionally shared those articles with the faculty and staff advisory group and sometimes with the entire staff.

The listserve provided one outlet for Nick's self-reflections. So that his ideas would not get away from him, Nick began keeping a diary. He tried hard to write at least a line a day about what worked, what didn't work, what puzzled him, or what he would like to do. Some days he just couldn't seem to put something in writing. No week went by without notes. The very act of writing seemed to make things more important, more memorable, and more doable. One of those ideas was to form a book club among the staff. Nick decided to select up to four books about change in education that he and interested others in the school would read and discuss over the next school year. Maybe he could get every member of the advisory council to participate and model good discussion for others. Then the group might grow. Perhaps even long-time devotees of Whitney would begin to question "how we do things around here."

9

PLANNING

Organizations do not improve spontaneously, and schools are no exception to this rule. Constant improvement depends on the expertise of our leaders. When we discussed the notion of becoming expert in the introduction, we described two drivers: one a novice, the other an expert. The expert drove with an intuitive rather than strictly cognitive sense of the right things to do. Throughout this book we have described and you have reflected upon ways to integrate knowing, thinking about, and doing that will help you develop the intuitive radar of an expert.

BECOMING A SCHOOL LEADERSHIP EXPERT: A CAREER LONG ENDEAVOR

Being expert requires that you stay on top of the game. Experts who do not continue to learn, practice, and stretch their capabilities do not remain expert very long. Each of us can think of someone once considered expert who is now considered obsolete. People say things like, "Why doesn't he just retire?" and "I hope I know enough to quit while I'm still on top." This chapter is entitled "Planning," but it is not about trendy and frequently abandoned types of planning. Instead, this chapter is about planning ways in which you and your school can continue to learn and be always on the journey toward expert. This chapter is about institutionalizing self-reflection and renewal for yourself and for your organization.

The idea that principals and schools need to plan to learn continually in order to achieve is not new. You have heard the phrases "community of learners" and "lifelong learners." Unfortunately, these phrases have been so often used and misused that their meanings may have become lost in the babble of trendy reform discourse. Don't let them become clichés for you. Planning for renewal is about living the ideas embodied in those phrases. If you as a leader and your school are to thrive, you must plan for learning to become a way of life for everyone who contributes to your school's daily life.

Studies indicate that many professions, including those in education, are subject to midlife and midcareer trauma and burnout (Elsass & Ralston, 1989; Krupp, 1983; Levinson, Darrow, Lelin, Levinson, & McKee, 1978; Lortie, 1975; Noe, 1988; Schein, 1978; Sheehy, 1976). Compounding the midcareer dilemma for principals is the lack of connection between the preservice education they received as graduate students and their current positions (Bridges, 1977; Murphy & Hallinger, 1987). In addition, schools have invested few resources in the continuing professional development of principals (Kranyik & Edgar, 1987).

Becoming a school leadership expert requires that you strive continually to develop skills necessary to being effective. Unfortunately, skills development is very difficult for principals. The nature of their preservice preparation may have separated theory from practice. The nature of their career path to administrative positions may have relied more on networks and visibility than on demonstration of current expertise. Many people who enter leadership positions do so long after they have completed their preservice training. Their preparatory programs may be completely disconnected from the work they end up doing years after graduation. Even if your preparatory program is appropriate at the time you complete it, much of its content is dated by the time you reach midcareer (Kranyik and Edgar, 1987). Opportunities to gain new knowledge and skills are rare, unless you are in an unusual situation. In addition, international, national, state, and local calls for changes in the organization, governance, and leadership of schools constantly require you to reexamine your role.

It is possible that you will be a principal for 10, 15, 20, or even more years. Staying current, maintaining motivation, and fighting burnout will be major challenges for you (Krupp, 1983; Schein, 1978). Internal conflicts arise as you experience public and self-inflicted pressure to "improve" schools. Your own professional education may work against you as you pressure yourself to live up to an idealized set of heroic standards (Bridges, 1977). At some point you are likely to question your assumptions about self, career, needs and values, relationships, and options (Schein, 1978). At the same time, others in your school, who have worked hard in good faith to improve, may also question the worth of their work. You need a renewal plan so that your capacity to learn and grow exceeds your capacity to give up in the face of never ending challenges.

Motivating yourself and others to constantly seek expertise requires more than repeated training in "one best way" to communicate mission, manage curriculum, supervise teaching, monitor student progress, and create a positive learning climate. Shaping new activities, behaviors, or actions requires consciously planning to reflect on, act upon, and make the most of opportunities within the unique setting of your school.

LEADERSHIP TUTORIAL: A MODEL FOR PURSUING EXPERTISE

Your individual belief system represents a powerful basis for implementing change. Your philosophy and vision of what your school can be define both possibilities and barriers for change. Your development as an expert depends in large part on embedding into your practice a means of constantly testing your belief system against your leadership behaviors.

One model development program, called the Leadership Tutorial (LT) Program, has been implemented on a statewide basis to help principals do just that. The use of the term *tutorial* suggests an individualized and context-embedded approach to leadership development. LT emphasizes features not often found in staff development programs for administrators: theory, individualization, and elements of "cognitive apprenticeship."

As administered under controlled research and development conditions, the LT Program combines assessment, feedback, and planning into a detailed agenda of specific activities during one or more academic years. The long-term nature of LT reflects a belief that significant change requires time and commitment.

In the original research-based Leadership Tutorial, a principal works with a tutor through several steps: assessment, reflection, planning, and implementation. Principals begin the LT process by completing a set of questionnaires designed to assess their instructional leadership skills, school climate, and motivation. The tutor helps the principal analyze and interpret the assessment data. Through on-site observation and interviews, the tutor gains insight into the school context in which the principal works and adds to possible interpretations of the assessment data. The tutor and the principal use the self-assessment, observation, and interview data to work with a school team. Together they develop a plan that reflects the principal's needs and matches training and development needs to available opportunities. Each plan addresses changes the principal wants to make within the context of his or her current work setting.

Once the plan is complete, the role of the tutor shifts from assessor/analyst to mentor/advisor. Studies of this mentoring role (Scott, Krug, & Ahadi, 1990) concluded that although the assessment framework was necessary for successful change, it was not sufficient. Support similar to that provided by the tutors during the assessment phase was also necessary for implementation of the development plan. Lack of support during implementation of the development plan decreased the likelihood of the plan being implemented during the normal course of a principal's job.

PURSUING EXPERTISE: PLANNING YOUR OWN LEADERSHIP TUTORIAL

Engaging a tutor for two or more years of assessment, reflection, planning, and implementation is expensive. On the other hand, if you have been reading and discussing this book with a colleague as we suggested, you are already engaged in the leadership tutorial, minus the overhead. If you have read the book alone, you might want to soon seek a colleague whom you respect and trust to slowly reread and experience the self-assessments in each chapter and to discuss Elizabeth's and Nick's experiences with you.

Research on the LT gives us good reason for recommending that you use this book as a guide to improving your leadership in the company of another. Planning for continuous learning, reflection, and application will most likely be productive if you involve someone else, another professional. Few of us are able to maintain a course of self and organizational improvement in isolation from knowledgeable peers. Effective school improvement requires principals to work collaboratively with faculty, staff, and others. However, this collaboration still lacks the professional perspective provided by a peer who has faced similar challenges as a designated school leader. Research on the Leadership Tutorial found that a tutor was essential to implementation of the plan (Scott et al., 1990).

Another important research finding was that both the principals and their tutors benefited from their participation in the LT program (Ashby, 1991). You and a colleague will both benefit from sharing your reactions to the self-assessment exercises. The conversations triggered by your self-assessments will lead to shared insights about how you work and how you might work in your schools.

Studies of the LT found that reflective conversations with someone who understands principals' working contexts were necessary for changes in principals' perceptions and behaviors. Self-assessment was necessary for successful change, but it was not sufficient. Support like that provided by the tutors during assessment was also necessary for implementation of the development plan. Lack of support during the implementation of the development plan decreased the likelihood of the plan being implemented during the normal course of a principal's job.

Working with a colleague will enable you to forge links between your knowledge of the principalship and the ways in which you can translate your knowledge into action. As collegial tutors, you can help each other refine your perceptions about school leadership and ways you could be a more expert school leader. Just as tutors' influences on the principals contributed to emergence of a sense of professional renewal, you and a colleague can work together so that professional growth and renewal stay ahead of burnout. Together you can decrease your feelings of isolation and expand your information networks.

How do you go about starting? First, find a trusted principal colleague who you know is as interested in continual development as you are. If you have truly identified such a person, persuading your peer to engage with you in extended self-study won't be difficult. If you work in an area where development of extraordinary principals is a clear priority, you might even suggest formation of a peer support group. The group would meet regularly to discuss the subjects of mission, culture and climate, curriculum, student achievement, and staff supervision. Use the self-assessments and the experiences of Nick and Elizabeth to kick off your conversations. As your meetings and conversations with another progress, include other rich resources to help you learn more about each area. Begin with some of the scholarly works referenced in this book, included in the syllabi of graduate courses, displayed on colleagues' shelves, or reviewed in educational periodicals.

Read each chapter and complete the related self-assessment. Do so thoughtfully and be honest with yourself. Sometimes it may be appropriate to consult with teachers, students, or others in your school to get other points of view regarding the assessment items as well. If you ignored our earlier suggestion, now may be a good time to begin a journal. Your journal can be something as simple as a ring binder or spiral notebook of convenient size in which you write answers to the self-assessments and record thoughts about why you selected the answers you did. The more technological among you may be more comfortable with an electronic journal. Whatever form it takes, you may also find the journal a handy place to keep notes about events of each school day that cause you concern, catch you by surprise, or make you think about the efficacy of your usual practices.

Another useful tool is the use of e-mail, if connectivity is possible. Keep your journal on a disk or hard drive. Excerpt portions of the journal and send them off to your collegial tutor for further reflection and comment. Electronic connections make corresponding pen pal-style with a colleague possible on a daily basis and encourage us to tend to our professional needs daily rather than occasionally.

As you complete your reflections on each chapter, jot notes regarding how you might change your behavior and the practices in your school so that your school begins to resemble your vision more closely. How can you put into place the beliefs and practices you have examined? How can you and your school come to operate more "expertly"?

After you have finished the book, review the data from your self-assessments and the notes you have made. In conversation with your tutor, summarize what you have learned about yourself and your school. Consider the various possible reasons you and your school behave as you do, especially when those behaviors seem to contradict your vision and philosophy.

Generate a list of things you would like to know more about before planning ways to change practices. How can this information be acquired? Your study of school records might identify some of the information. A third party might more reasonably gather other data you need. This is a role your tutor can play. Still other data might best be gathered by a professional researcher or by a study team in your school. Combine your understandings of the data gathered with the data from your self-assessment to make a personal plan for pursuing expertise. Share data with others in the school to engage your entire team in developing expert expectations for constant improvement throughout your school.

Implement your plans with the continued support of a collegial tutor or tutor group. Constantly engage in conversations about what is happening, what is not happening, and how it is working. Use these conversations as a means of testing assumptions, checking perceptions, and developing strategies for dealing with emerging problems. Constantly assess and fine-tune your plan so that learning to learn while doing becomes an accepted way of doing business. Revisit the assessment instruments regularly and check your responses against your initial answers as one means of monitoring changes in the ways you think about your role as principal.

RECOMMENDATIONS FOR
CONTINUAL DEVELOPMENT

We believe that investing in continuous professional development of principals is an investment in school change. You may get support from your local school district, your professional association, and your state education agency. This support usually takes the form of informational meetings, legal briefings, or professional development opportunities available as a means of meeting requirements for continued certification. None of these opportunities ensures that you will learn anything or that you have the potential to be an exciting and inspiring leader. Only you can do that by taking charge of your professional development and motivating those with whom you work to do the same.

Following is a list of ideas for taking charge of your developing expertise. Feel free to add to it.

- Attend group presentations to learn of changes in laws and regulations, new administrative tools and techniques, or new research.

- Join one or more professional associations and subscribe to their literature as an ongoing means of staying in touch with changes in legal requirements, administrative technologies, emerging research, and recommended practice. (Begin by considering these well-respected professional associations: National Association of Elementary School Principals; National Association of Secondary School Principals; Association for Supervision and Curriculum Development, National Staff Development.)

- Find a learner-partner who might serve as a collegial tutor. Commit to a long-term, one-on-one approach to studying yourselves, your schools, and educational literature.

- Participate in formal and informal administrator networks. Formal networks include regional meetings hosted by state associations and intermediate service units. Informal networks arise from these and other gatherings for various purposes, such as discussion of sporting conference schedules, special education cooperative business, or staff development conferences.

- Go back to school. University coursework provides a ready-made opportunity to network with others interested in becoming experts. Focus on learning how to collect, analyze, and use data to improve the decision-making capacity of your school.

- Mentor others who should become administrators. Help them acquire experiences that will provide them a sense of accomplishment and a sense of the potential good they can accomplish if they continue to study and develop themselves as leaders.

- Work with other experienced principals to provide novice administrators with support during their

first year or two. Support is especially necessary
for those whose administrative preparation occurred long before they began their first principalship.
The greater the time lag, the greater the need for
support!

♦ Get in contact with universities that take pride in
their administrator preparation programs. Learn
more about their work. Offer your school as a potential placement site for aspiring principals seeking intern experiences. Volunteer to speak to classes
about the role and responsibilities of principals.
Teaching others is a sure means of continuing to
motivate yourself to learn.

♦ Explore ways of incorporating growth in expertise
in your school as an expectation. Establish book
groups to read and report on current educational
literature. Ask staff members to share news items
that have implications for schools at staff meetings.
Use case studies and simulations as safe ways for
faculty, staff, parents, and students to work together
on sharing values, solving problems, and resolving
conflicts. Provide opportunities for teachers to visit
other classrooms, in their school and in others. Find
ways to empower faculty, staff, students, and parents to gather and analyze data about their school.

♦ Share your practice. Sharing takes several forms, including discussions of reflective journals and professional literature. Sharing may also take the form
of making local, regional, state and national presentations regarding effective practices. Although ap-
plying to lead a workshop or make a presentation
means putting a little ego on the line, the reward of
being validated is worth the risk.

Becoming expert requires that you push yourself to learn
and practice continually. You must motivate others to become
experts as well, in large part by your example.

You will have to work very hard to be highly invested in the
role of principal without letting the job overwhelm and con-
sume you. Even today, in a time when so much is made about

the importance of the principalship, too many principals say, "I don't have time to read," or, "I don't have any interest in going back to school." Principals who do not have time to read and discuss professional literature clearly signal to others in the school that continuing to learn and develop is not a high priority.

Remember the second chapter in which we addressed philosophy and vision? All the words in the world mean nothing if you contradict them by your actions. Where you put your time communicates your true values. If you do not have time to read, to go back to school, to participate in professional associations, to attend regional workshops, you are communicating that professional development is unnecessary.

This is one of those times that folk wisdom will again prevail. You cannot expect the people with whom you work to "do as I say, not as I do." Your school needs and deserves an exceptional principal whose actions reflect your values, who communicates mission, monitors student progress, promotes a productive school climate, supports staff, and focuses on curriculum.

ELIZABETH COMMITS TO CONTINUOUS PROFESSIONAL DEVELOPMENT

At the end of her second year at Central, Elizabeth was just as tired as she had been at the end of the first year. Senior Play Night presented significant "blow up" potential since the farce poked fun at administrators, staff, teachers, and under class students. During graduation Elizabeth spent a great deal of time checking robes for contraband, insisting that feet be covered by shoes and socks, and praying that the valedictorian would present the agreed upon speech. Elizabeth was ready for vacation. Unfortunately, the vacation had to wait while the girl's softball team made an unprecedented run at the state title. By the time softball tournaments were over, a small summer school (which included a few "graduated" seniors) was in full-swing Monday through Thursday mornings for four weeks.

Even so, when Elizabeth caught her breath in late June and assessed the progress of the past two years, she was pleased. There was no doubt in her mind that both she and the entire school had come a long way. No longer did a feeling of being disenfranchised rule. Although Elizabeth could not claim that everyone was on board, she could safely claim that a sense of team and dedication to a single purpose had certainly developed and had begun to guide judgments. Data had become more important than personality or idiosyncratic style in determining the outcomes of crucial decisions.

In February, Elizabeth had promised herself she would find some means of renewing her intellectual and professional energies over the summer. She had applied to and been accepted at a professional development institute sponsored by a national organization. Although spending a week on a university campus to attend the institute was expensive, Elizabeth had decided to go even without financial support from her district. Much to her surprise, the district agreed to cover the enrollment fee, her lodging, and her mileage if she would drive.

The institute was wonderful. Each morning she awoke early and ran with a small group of enthusiasts who enjoyed the feeling of freedom running into the sunrise gave them. She replayed the conversations of the group as she showered. By Friday morning, their last run together, members of the group had shared intimate details of their professional highs and lows. They had brainstormed long lists of potential ways to confront challenges waiting for them when they returned home. They exchanged telephone, address, and e-mail information. Everyone knew that the likelihood they would stay in touch was slim, but they felt that even if they made contact only irregularly, a safe support group was out there.

Elizabeth paid rapt attention to most of the speakers who met with institute members each morning and evening. Only one seemed to her a waste of time. This was mostly because his ideas seemed based on ideals of American society and families that Elizabeth simply could not accept. Even so, he at least made her angry enough that during the afternoon discussion Elizabeth found herself better able than ever before to express her values and philosophy of education. Words describing what she believed principals should do and work for flowed as she and others debated the speaker's ideas. Maybe he wasn't a waste of time after all.

Most important, Elizabeth met a colleague whose ideas intrigued her. When she had initially learned that she would have a roommate, Elizabeth almost turned around for home. Much to her surprise, Pam had turned out to be a delight. Pam

was about six years older than Elizabeth and the only other female secondary principal Elizabeth had ever met. Pam's experiences included being a dean of students, an athletic director,
and an assistant principal before being named principal four
years ago. Pam's new job, as principal of a major city high
school, would move her only 35 miles from Elizabeth.

Elizabeth arranged to help Pam, her three children, and her
husband move into their new home. At last Elizabeth had met
someone with whom she could talk about her profession without feeling competitive or under constant scrutiny. As the principal of the smallest high school in her district, and as the only
female principal at the secondary level, she had been reluctant
to share too many of her concerns with other administrators in
her district. She kept telling herself that she would have to get
over that and find ways to engage in sharing conversations in
her home district. In the meantime, she had found Pam who, as
a new member of her own district, welcomed an outlet for
"safe" conversation outside her new circle of colleagues.

The start of school consumed both principals, particularly
Pam, who was getting used to a new system. Even so, they
scheduled regular times to get together for dinner and conversation. Once Pam's e-mail was up and running, they corre-
sponded electronically nearly daily. Elizabeth maintained a
record of their e-mail in a word processing file for easy reference. She had a feeling their correspondence would be very
helpful in the future as they reflected on where they had been
as well as where they were going. Occasional telephone conversations added to their collegial relationship.

Throughout the fall, between football games and golf season, Elizabeth shared with Pam the various types of processes
Central had experienced the past two years. She talked through
some of the data and the areas on which everyone had agreed to
place particular emphasis. She expressed concern about running out of steam and the need to institutionalize change as a
normal course of doing the school's business. Pam offered to
spend a couple of days in Elizabeth's school after the winter
holiday season. This way she could provide Elizabeth with
some feedback about how the culture and climate appeared to a
stranger. In exchange, she asked, would Pam spend a couple of
days at her building observing a new team-teaching approach to
freshman core subjects? In particular, could Elizabeth act as a

process observer at team meetings, helping the team understand how team members worked together and how they might learn to work together more effectively?

CONCLUSION

Elizabeth and Pam are exploring a form of collegial tutoring. Perhaps, as their relationship develops, they will be able to use tools provided by this book and other resources to help each other with the leadership role each must play in constantly improving schools. The same may be true for Nick and his expanding support network.

Your challenge is to find a support system so that you do not work in isolation. Support may be as near as the other professionals in your building and district. You may feel supported by those nearest to you but unable to have completely honest and open discussions with them about some of the issues you have uncovered as you worked through this book. That is both understandable and common. Begin by looking for a like soul at conferences, meetings, and in graduate classes. Perhaps you will be part of initiating an ongoing support and discussion group.

The principalship is one of the most exciting jobs in education. It can be the loneliest. It can be the center of attention. Most important, the principalship is key to the ability of our educational system to unlock human potential for learning and for life. As principal, you are responsible for the learning of the adults and children whom you presume to lead. Lead them to excellence as you pursue the goal of becoming expert.

It is a shameful thing to be weary of inquiry when what we search for is excellence.

—Cicero

REFERENCES

Ashby, D.E. (1991). *Study of project mentoring as a method of administrative renewal and professional development.* Unpublished doctoral dissertation, Southern Illinois University, Carbondale, IL.

Austin, G.R. (1979). Exemplary schools and the search for effectiveness. *Educational Leadership, 37,* 10–12, 14.

Barth, R.S. (1981). The principal as staff developer. *Journal of Education, 163*(2), 125–143.

Barth, R.S. (1990). *Improving schools from within.* San Francisco: Jossey-Bass Publishers.

Blase, J.J. (1987). Dimensions of effective school leadership: The teacher's perspective. *American Educational Research Journal, 24,* 4, 589–610.

Brandt, R. (1987). On student leadership: A conversation with Richard Andrews. *Educational Leadership, 45*(1), 9–16.

Braskamp, L.A., and Maehr, M.L. (1985). *SPECTRUM: An organizational development tool.* Champaign, IL: MetriTech, Inc.

Braskamp, L.A., and Maerh, M.L. (1988a). *School administrator assessment survey.* Champaign, IL: MetriTech, Inc.

Braskamp, L.A., and Maerh, M.L. (1988b). *Instructional climate inventory: Forms.* Champaign, IL: MetriTech, Inc.

Bridges, E.M. (1977). The nature of leadership. In L. Cunningham, W. Hack, and R. Nystrands (Eds.), *Educational administration: The developing decade.* Berkeley: McCutchan.

Brieve, F.J. (1972). Secondary principals as instructional leaders. *NASSP Bulletin, 55,* 11–15.

Brookover, W., Beamer, L., Efthim, H., et al. (1982). *Creating effective schools.* Holmes Beach, FL: Learning Publications, Inc.

Costa, A.L., and Liebmann, R. (1995). Process is as important as content. *Educational Leadership, 52*(6), 23.

Dwyer, D.C. (1985). *Contextual antecedents of instructional leadership*. Paper presented at the Annual Meeting of the American Educational Research Association, Chicago, IL.

Eberts, R.W., and Stone, J.A. (1988). Student achievement in public schools: Do principals make a difference? *Economics of Education Review, 7*(3), 291–299.

Edmonds, R. (1979). Effective schools for the urban poor. *Educational Leadership, 37*, 15–27.

Edwards, M.A. (1995). Growth is the name of the game. *Educational Leadership, 52*(6), 72–74.

Elsass, P.M., and Ralston, D.A. (1989). Individual responses to the stress of career plateauing. *Journal of Management, 15*, 35–47.

English, Fenwick W. (1988). *Curriculum auditing*. Lancaster, PA: Technomic Publishing Co.

French, W.L., and Bell, C.H. Jr. (1990). *Organization development* (4th ed.). Englewood Cliffs, NJ: Prentice Hall.

Fullan, M.G. (1988). *What's worth fighting for in the principalship?* Toronto, ON: Ontario Public School Teacher's Federation.

Gandal, M. (for the AFT). (1995). Not all standards are created equal. *Educational Leadership, 52*(6), 16–21.

Hallinger, P. (1984). *Principal instructional management rating scale*. New York: Leading Development Associates.

Hallinger, P., and Hausman, C. (1994). From Attila the Hun to Mary had a little lamb: Principal role ambiguity in restructured schools. In J. Murphy and K. Seashore Louis (Eds.) *Reshaping the principalship: Insights from transformational reform efforts*. Thousand Oaks, CA: Corwin Press, Inc.

Hallinger, P., and Murphy, J. (1985). Assessing the instructional management behavior of principals. *The Elementary School Journal, 86(2)*, 217–242.

Hartzell, G.N. (1995). Effective supervision: Planning evaluation conferences with support staff members. *The High School Magazine, 2*(3), 26–29.

Hoy, W.K., and Miskel, C.G. (1987). *Educational administration theory, research and practice.* (3rd ed.) New York: Random House.

Ianni, F.A. (1979). Field research and educational administration. In. R. Barnhardt, J. Chilcott, and H. Wolcott (Eds.) *Anthropology and educational administration.* Tucson: Impresora Sahuaro, 375–408.

Kachur, D., Goodall, B., and Ashby, D. (1990). Linking staff development to teacher observation. *Curriculum and Staff Development, 7,* 12–15.

Killion, J.P., Huddleston, J.P., and Claspell, M.A. (1989). People developer: A new role for principals. *The Journal of Staff Development, 10*(1), 2–7.

Kranyik, R., and Edgar, W. (1987). Life begins at 46: Model for the self-development and renewal of principals. In D. Hagstron (Ed.), *Reflections 1987.* Boston, MA: Harvard Principals Center.

Krug, S.E. (1989). Leadership and learning: A measurement-based approach for analyzing school effectiveness and developing effective school leaders. In C. Ames and M.L. Maehr (Eds.). *Advances in motivation and achievement, 6,* 249–277. Greenwich, CT: JAI Press.

Krupp, J. (1983). Mentoring: A means of sparking school personnel. *Journal of Counseling and Development, 64,* 154–155.

Leithwood, K.A. (1987). Using the principal profile to assess performance. *Educational Leadership, 45,* 63–68.

Leithwood, K.A. (1990). The principal's role in teacher development. In *Changing school culture through staff development, 1990 ASCD Yearbook.* Alexandria, VA: Association for Supervision and Curriculum Development, 71–90.

Levinson, D.J. (with Darrow, C.N., Klein, E.B., Levinson, M.H., and McKee, B.) (1978). *The seasons of a man's life.* New York: Alfred A. Knopf.

Lortie, D.C. (1975). *School-teacher.* Chicago, IL: The University of Chicago Press.

Maehr, M.D., and Ames, R. (1988). *Instructional leadership inventory.* Champaign, IL: MetriTech.

Maehr, M.L., and Braskamp, L. (1986). *The motivation factor: A theory of personal investment.* Lexington, MA: D.C. Heath and Company.

Maehr, M.L., Braskamp, L., and Ames, R. (1988). *Instructional climate inventory: Form T.* Champaign, IL: MetriTech.

Maehr, M.L., and Parker, S.A. (1993). A tale of two schools—and the primary task of leadership. *Phi Delta Kappan, 75,* 233–239.

Manasse, A.L. (1984). Principals as leaders of high performing systems. *Educational Leadership, 41*(5), 42–46.

Marcus, A.C. (1976). *Administrative leadership in a sample of successful schools from the national evaluation of the emergency school aid act.* Santa Monica, CA: System Development Corporation and Washington, DC: U.S. Office of Education.

Martin, W.J., and Willower, D.J. (1981). The managerial behavior of high school principals. *Educational Administration Quarterly, 17*(1), 69–90.

McCall, J. (1994). *The principal's edge.* Princeton Junction, NJ: Eye on Education.

McEvoy, B. (1987). Everyday acts: How principals influence development of their staffs. *Educational Leadership, 44*(5), 73–77.

Morris, V.C., Crawson, R.L., Hurwitz, E., and Porter-Gehrie, C. (1981). *The urban principal: Discretionary decision making in a large educational organization.* Washington, DC: National Institute of Education (ERIC Document Service No. 207178).

Murphy, J., and Hallinger, P. (1987). *Approaches to administrative training.* Albany, NY: State University of New York Press.

Murphy, J. (1992). *The landscape of leadership preparation: Reframing the education of school administrators.* Newbury Park, CA: Corwin Press.

National Policy Board for Educational Administration. (1993). *Principals for our changing schools.* S.D. Thompson (Ed.). Fairfax: VA: National Policy Board for Educational Administration.

Noe, R.A. (1988). An investigation of the determinants of successful assigned mentoring relationships. *Personnel Psychology, 41,* 457–480.

Peters, T. (1994). *The Tom Peters seminar: Crazy times call for crazy organization.* New York: Vintage Books.

Peters, T.J., and Waterman, R.H. (1984). *In search of excellence.* New York: Warner Books.

Quinn, R.E. (1988). *Beyond rational management.* San Francisco: Jossey-Bass.

Regional Lab Reports (1992). *Looking at the personal and professional lives of teachers: Michael Huberman speaks on teacher life cycles.* Andover, MA: Regional Laboratory for Educational Improvements of the Northeast and Islands.

Resnick, L.B., and Nolan, K.J. (1995). Where in the world are world class standards? *Educational Leadership, 52*(6), 6–11.

Ryan, J.M. (1995). *Current practices and procedures in testing and measurement.* Reston, VA: National Association of Secondary School Administrators.

Rudman, C. (1996). *Frames of reference.* Princeton, NJ: Peterson's/Pacesetter Books.

Rutherford, W.L., Hord, S.M., and Huling, L.L. (1983). *An analysis of terminology used for describing leadership.* Austin: Research and Development Center for Teacher Education, University of Texas.

Sarason, S. (1990). *The predictable failure of school reform: Can we change course before it's too late?* San Francisco: Jossey-Bass.

Schein, E.H. (1978). *Career dynamics: Matching individual and organizational needs.* Reading, MA: Addison-Wesley.

Scott, C.K., Krug, S.E., and Ahadi, S.A. (1990). *Current issues and research findings in the study of school leadership.* Champaign, IL: National Center for School Leadership.

Senge, P.M. (1990). The leader's new work: Building learning organizations. *Sloan Management Review, 32,* 7–19.

Sheehy, G. (1976). *Passages.* New York: E.P. Dutton.

Sparks, D., and Loucks-Horsley, S. (1989). Five models of staff development for teachers. *Journal of Staff Development, 10*(4), 40–57.

Stronge, J.H., and Tucker, P.D. (1995). The principal's role in evaluating professional support personnel. *NASSP Practitioner, 21*(3).

Uebbing, S.J. (1995). Planning for technology. *Executive Educator, 17*(11), 21–23,

Weber, G. (1971). *Inner-city children can be taught to read: Four successful schools*. Washington, DC: Council for Basic Education.

Weisbord, M.R. (1976). Diagnosing your organization: A "six box" learning exercise. Wynnewood, PA: Organization Research and Development.

Wellisch, J.B., MacQueen, A.H., Carriere, R.A., and Duck, G.A. (1978). School management and organization in successful schools. *Sociology of Education, 51*, 211–221.

Zepeda, , S.J. (1995). How to ensure positive responses in classroom observations. *Tips for Principals*. May. Reston, VA: National Association of Secondary School Principals.

Zlatos, B. (1993). Outcome-based outrage. *Executive Educator. 15*(12), 12–16.